# Wander Woman

# Wander Woman

*A testimony of resilience, dream making, and a 100-mile race*

Dawn Nunes

First paperback edition
First Printing, 2024
ISBN 978-1-0685625-0-1
Independently published

# Glen, Josh, Jen, & Storm

*Thanks for loving my crazy.*

# Paul Brenton

*Aroo! Dreams are made of this!*

*With God, all things are possible.*

This book would not have been possible without the incredible friends and family that I have been blessed with in my life. Thank you for believing in me, especially when I didn't believe in myself. After three years, this dream has turned into reality.

# Table of Contents

*Periodisation Training: A training program with progressive phases leading towards the build-up of a goal race.*

Dear Dream Chaser

Never give up on your dreams.

Fight for them.

Work for them.

Surround yourself with your tribe.

You will achieve so much more

              than you can ever imagine.

Your fellow adventurer,

Dawn

# Resilient

**Capable of withstanding or recovering quickly
from difficult conditions**

A hundred-miler: one hundred and sixty kilometres on a trail with over 8,000 metres of climbing in the Cape Town mountains, South Africa—an inaugural race. But let's journey back to the beginning, to my lowest of lows, which ignited this daunting, larger-than-life dream.

Three years ago, in an instant, it seemed like my life of running was cruelly snatched away from me. A second before, my hamstring had utterly detached from my pelvis, leaving me lost, broken, desperate, and confused. I found myself unable to run; I cried, screamed, prayed, and wrestled with this. And to top it all off, I couldn't go for that run to release my frustrations as I normally would. Then came surgery, marking the beginning of my healing journey. At that time, I didn't realise that undergoing the operation to reattach my hamstring to the ischial bone in my pelvis, navigating through the rehabilitation as both a physiotherapist and a runner while witnessing the slow progress, was the commencement of a remarkable journey of resilience and personal growth.

This all unfolded while I was simultaneously launching my private physiotherapy practice, balancing family life as a mum and wife, and navigating the complexities introduced by the arrival of a global pandemic. As COVID-19 spread, it forever altered the world as we knew it.

## The Beginning of a Daring Dream: A Hundred-Miler Trail Race

As someone who had run multiple marathons, including Comrades and Two Oceans Marathon, this was something new. I had never contemplated attempting that distance; however, it soon became all-consuming. The idea gradually took root as one trail race led to another until the Ultra Trail Cape Town (UTCT) 100 miler 2022 emerged as the ultimate dream race.

I want to motivate you to share your stories and reignite your dreams. You, too, can dismantle the barriers you've constructed. While time and commitment present challenges, prioritising our aspirations, supported by a network that encourages and holds us accountable, ensures that drive and satisfaction ensue. This is a brief look into my life, confronting physical challenges and embracing life's transformations, bolstered by the unwavering support of my treasured family and friends.

I quickly understood that my journey extended beyond running; it was an emotional odyssey. It revealed how I adapted and adjusted, growing resilient throughout my preparation for my most significant race yet. This story illustrates how, against all odds, determination can overcome formidable barriers. It speaks to how the transformative challenges I encountered catalysed my passion and dream.

## The Daunting Task Ahead

I find myself both nervous and scared. The trepidation isn't solely about embarking on a new challenge with increased mileage but also about the vulnerability of sharing my journey with you. This story offers a candid glimpse into my life, charting a course from the depths of severe injury to the pinnacle of achieving a dream amidst the ever-evolving challenges that life's mountains present.

My resolve to make the 100-miler my driving force was unwavering, compelling me to place one foot in front of the other, even when the temptation to abandon my training and dreams loomed large. Often, that's precisely what's required:

a simple, determined succession of steps. Repeat as necessary.

What you're about to read lies my tale of perseverance—how, even in the most profound despair, I managed to take one more step.

# Phase 1: Base

**Comrades Ultra Marathon**

"Dad, I can't run anymore."

"That's okay, but we'll finish the 5 km. We'll walk to a pole, run a pole, then run until we're done." We found key targets to break up the run into a walk/run every few hundred metres.

This remains one of my earliest running memories. At the tender age of five, I learned a valuable lesson: I started too fast and soon had nothing left, with a long way to go for my young legs. Yet, my father was undeterred. He was determined that we would complete the 5 km we had set out to do, and indeed, we did. The discipline my father demonstrated in training consistently and ensuring we finished what we started has formed the cornerstone of my approach to training and life.

My father, Peter Durant Anderson, was a seasoned runner, completing 11 Comrades Ultramarathons (90km) and three Two Oceans Ultramarathons (56km). On his birthday, when I was 16, I promised him, penned in his birthday card, that I would run the Comrades Ultramarathon in his honour once I was old enough—at least 20 years old. At that moment, I perhaps didn't grasp the full significance of my commitment. Yet, I've always held a deep respect for keeping my word. I made this vow to my father earnestly, and I was fully committed to honouring it.

## When the Dawn Breaks

Hockey had been a significant part of my life for as long as I can remember. The team's camaraderie, intricate plays, and a shared determination to overcome challenges made it my first love. Running played a supportive role, enhancing my fitness for hockey. Despite enjoying cross country and regular runs, the adrenaline rush from hockey was unparalleled. However, everything changed on the 26th of April 1999, as I left hockey practice. Out of nowhere, a car collided with my motorbike. The impact launched me into the air, over the car's bonnet, and I landed on my back in the middle of the road.

## Time seemed to freeze.

I was shattered, both physically and emotionally. I sustained hairline fractures in my C3/C4 neck vertebrae and needed seven stitches in my left knee. Wearing a full neck brace for four months drastically limited my mobility and brought immense pain, especially at night. All of this was done while completing my final year at school. This accident robbed me of the chance to play for the provincial hockey team and stripped me of my captaincy. The devastation was overwhelming. Yet, in this dark time, the warmth and love from my friends and family were palpable. Their visits, the flowers, and the gifts they brought me helped cushion the blow of my losses. I even tried to watch a hockey game, hoping it might lift my spirits, but the sight of the field only deepened my sorrow, stirring up feelings of grief, frustration, and a sense of injustice. Why did this tragedy strike just as my dreams were beginning to materialise?

## A Stop Gap

My love for an active lifestyle, passion for working with people and fascination with the human body and its movements naturally drew me towards physiotherapy as a career path. Unfortunately, my academic performance in the final year didn't meet the entry requirements for the universities I had applied to. Faced with this setback, I opted for a gap year dedicated to travel and work to broaden my horizons.

I planned to use this time to enhance my application with worldly experiences before reapplying to study physiotherapy. True to my strategy, I reapplied to four universities for the physiotherapy program and received two acceptance offers. Ultimately, I chose to begin my physiotherapy studies at the University of the Western Cape (UWC) in January 2001.

## Embracing Innovation and Opportunity

My parents have always been prudent with finances, firmly believing in living within their means rather than relying on credit. In line with this philosophy, we struck a practical arrangement: I could live at home throughout my four years of study, provided I repay them for the university fees afterwards.

### Thinking creatively was essential.

Thankfully, through my mother's birth in Nottingham, I was eligible for a British passport, opening doors to work in the United Kingdom. Each Christmas break during my university years, I seized the opportunity to work in the UK for six to nine weeks, earning pounds to finance my education. These stints were an adventure, taking on any job available, despite coinciding with the British winter's chill as South Africa enjoyed its warm summer days. Though it meant missing family and friends during the festive season, the goal of clearing my university fees to emerge debt-free as a qualified physiotherapist kept me focused and driven.

## Navigating New Chapters and Connections

Imagine a scene where fourth-year physiotherapy students collaborate within the bustling environment of Groote Schuur Hospital's cardiothoracic ICU. Two of these students hailed from the University of the Western Cape (UWC), while the other two studied at the University of Cape Town (UCT). It was in this clinical setting that I first crossed paths with Glen. The tale of our meeting has since been told in several versions, varying slightly depending on the narrator. However, as the author of this account, I'll share my version of events.

Admittedly, my initial attempt to initiate a conversation with Glen featured something other than the smoothest opening lines. I blurted out, "Are you the guy from the magazine?" Glen responded with a mix of surprise and denial, insisting he had never appeared in any magazine. I elaborated, explaining that I recognised him from a physiotherapy magazine where he was mentioned as the class representative for his year. It even featured him in one of the articles. His response? A blank stare, leaving an impression that would mark the beginning of an unexpected journey.

**Embarking Together**

In keeping with my proactive nature, I promised to bring the magazine the next day to prove my point, which I indeed did. Glen was taken aback, having never seen the picture and not knowing it had been published, and that moment marked the beginning of our journey together. Our conversation flowed effortlessly despite my distaste for my ICU block, which Glen seemed to navigate with a serene and composed demeanour. Ironically, it turned out to be the clinical block in which I excelled the most, despite my aversion to the constant beeping of machines and the meticulous checks required before moving a patient.

A significant connection for me was discovering that Glen shared my Christian faith, an essential trait I sought in a partner. As our final year of studies progressed, amidst the hectic schedules, we found time to nurture our budding friendship, which gradually blossomed into a romantic relationship.

After a 19-hour drive from Cape Town to Durban, what better way to conclude the journey than with an engagement? True to this spontaneous spirit, we married on the 14th of January 2006 in Cape Town. Our wedding was a modest affair, surrounded by a close-knit circle of friends and family, followed by barn dancing. The initial days of our honeymoon were spent in Stellenbosch, staying at a picturesque wine estate, before we journeyed along the Garden Route. With no fixed itinerary, we savoured the scenic beauty at our leisure, embracing the start of our shared life to enjoy each moment fully. Nine months into our marriage, we embarked on a new adventure, moving to the UK to explore and travel together.

## Charting a New Course

After nine months of marriage, our journey took a significant turn when we decided to relocate to the UK. Venturing into a new country as a newlywed couple presented challenges, but we navigated them together successfully. Securing a physiotherapy position at that time was daunting, yet we found our footing in Chester, northwest England. There, I had the opportunity to work at several esteemed physiotherapy clinics, including one at the Vauxhall factory. After spending four enriching years in the UK, a milestone was reached when Glen acquired his British passport, prompting us to contemplate returning to South Africa, fueled by the desire to start our family.

How does one decide to return to their homeland or shift countries entirely? We resorted to a straightforward decision-making strategy. We drew up a list, dividing a sheet of paper into two columns: one outlining the positives of moving back to South Africa and the other detailing the negatives. Beneath these, we listed the advantages and disadvantages of remaining in the UK. This exercise highlighted vital aspects such as family ties, the climate, travel opportunities, and potential financial implications. It became clear that the benefits of returning to South Africa surpassed the negatives, leading us to book our flights.

This systematic approach to decision-making has served me well, both for significant life changes and minor choices. It offers a structured way to evaluate all possibilities, visually laying out the pros and cons and guiding us toward a decision that might have felt overwhelming. Before our return to Durban, we quenched our wanderlust with a seven-week tour of Europe, ensuring we departed with no regrets and ready to embark on the next chapter of our lives.

## Returning with Heavy Hearts

Not long after settling back in our homeland, we were confronted with the heart-wrenching news that our beloved friend, David, was in the final stages of his battle with cancer. I had first crossed paths with David at the Vauxhall plant, where I noticed a suspicious mole on his back and urged him to seek medical attention. Sadly, by the time the cancer was diagnosed, it was already advanced. Despite undergoing two surgeries aimed at excising the malignancy and initial hopes that it had been completely removed, the cancer had metastasized to his lymph nodes and swiftly spread throughout his body.

Compelled by a deep sense of friendship and the desire to support him in his final days, we decided to travel back to the UK that November. It was a sorrowful journey as we prepared to bid farewell to a dear friend. David's courageous fight came to an end shortly after our visit. His spirit and bravery continue to live on in our hearts, a lasting tribute embodied in our son, Joshua David Nunes, whom we named in his honour.

## Navigating New Beginnings and Challenges
Settling back in Durban by June 2011, we soon prepared for another significant life change. After moving into our new home in October, November brought the surprising yet delightful discovery that I was pregnant with our first child. The revelation came about unexpectedly over tea with my friend Jade when I complained about the milk tasting sour—a remark that made Jade question if I might be pregnant. Her intuition prompted me to take a pregnancy test, which confirmed her suspicions. My first scan, under the assumption I was 12 weeks along, astonishingly revealed I was already 19 weeks pregnant. In hindsight, the fatigue I had attributed to the demands of a new job and the move was, in fact, due to the pregnancy.

This posed a significant challenge. I had recently enrolled in a Masters in Sports Physiotherapy program, set to begin in January 2012, which required my presence in Cape Town for three separate weeks of lectures. My eligibility to fly while pregnant was narrowly within the timeframe allowed without needing a doctor's clearance—indeed, a stroke of fortune. At 28 weeks pregnant, I travelled to Cape Town to enrol and attend my first week of classes, staying with my parents during this period. Joshua David Nunes was born on the 7th of May 2012, and I continued to commute to Cape Town for lectures, with Joshua staying with my parents.

Balancing breastfeeding and academic commitments was challenging; I often had to save milk for these lecture periods, a task Joshua's feeding preferences made difficult. Eventually, my mother brought him to me for feedings during lunch breaks, a much-needed solution for both of us.

Juggling the roles of a new mother to a baby who struggled with sleep, a student committed to pursuing a masters, and managing household finances—with Glen working long hours at a rehabilitation centre—was an exhaustive endeavour. You might wonder why I chose to undertake my masters during such a demanding time. My rationale was straightforward: embarking on this academic journey would presumably be simpler with one child rather than two, as we hoped to expand our family further.

**Round Two**

In my third year, 2014, I submitted my dissertation by February, which was accepted by April. Concurrently, I was pregnant with our second child. This joy, however, was short-lived. At our nine-week scan, we discovered I had a blighted ovum. It's challenging to articulate the emotions of that period, a time not widely known among my acquaintances—not due to reluctance in sharing, but rather because I hadn't perceived it as particularly significant. Yet, the more I engage in conversations with other women, the more I recognise the importance of sharing my experience.

My gynaecologist explained the situation: the egg had been fertilised and had begun to develop but had failed to progress, resulting in an early miscarriage. There was a risk that the remnants could naturally expel, but to avoid potential complications, a D&C (dilation and curettage) was recommended to remove the tissue and prevent infection. Discovering the pregnancy only to face its loss so soon was devastating. The most profound moment of grief struck upon awakening from the procedure, the reality setting in that I was no longer carrying a child. I tried to console myself with the thought that it was perhaps for the best, yet a sense of emptiness lingered. My gynaecologist assured me that all looked well health-wise, advising me to wait for my next menstrual cycle before attempting to conceive again. Numerous questions and concerns flooded my mind, including fears of potential future miscarriages and contemplations of adoption. Glen's unwavering support was a pillar of strength throughout this tumultuous time.

Our fortune turned relatively quickly. Blessed with our son Joshua, who was then a vibrant two-year-old, we found ourselves expecting once again just a few weeks later. Jennifer Amy Nunes was born on the 12th of February 2015, bringing completeness to our family in a way we could have never anticipated.

## Back in the Game

Having completed my Masters in Sports Physiotherapy, I balanced part-time work between lecturing and private practice. My priorities began to shift. Six months later, Jennifer showed no further interest in breastfeeding, and I quickly saw the advantages of bottle-feeding. She flourished, and I was eager to return to my sporting life. Returning to hockey was my first step, followed by running again. The initial period was challenging. Battling with my fitness levels but driven by determination, I joined a local running group. The members were incredibly supportive, gradually helping me regain a respectable running pace.

My involvement with the club grew, and I set my sights on a significant goal. In October 2016, I entered my first marathon, laying the groundwork for an even more substantial challenge. I aimed to participate in the 2017 Comrades Marathon, a gruelling 90 km road race stretching from Pietermaritzburg to Durban. This began a new chapter in my athletic journey, filled with renewed goals and the excitement of rekindling my passion for running.

## First Comrades: The Ultimate Human Race

Qualifying for the Comrades Marathon, dubbed "The Ultimate Human Race," requires completing a standard marathon. My journey to this pinnacle event was marked by dedication and rigorous preparation.

## Build-up

My training regimen was consistent and demanding, incorporating road running six days a week. As the race approached, I intensified my efforts with double training sessions twice a week for two to three weeks, pushing my weekly mileage from 60-80 km to a peak of 120 km. This comprehensive program included track workouts, hill repeats, long, slow-distance weekend runs, and steady or easy runs during the week.

I adopted an early morning routine to accommodate this demanding schedule and minimise the impact on family life. Training commenced before dawn to ensure I could return by 6 am, aligning with my family's wake-up time. This allowed me an hour to ready myself, assist with the children, and manage school drop-offs by 7 am. My second daily session was either at lunch or after Glen returned home in the evening.

Weekend runs were also scheduled in the early hours, sometimes requiring me to wake at 3:30 am to complete runs by 6/7 am, especially for mid-week long runs extending to 20 km. Adequate rest was crucial; thus, my bedtime during peak training was between 8:30 pm and 9 pm.

Nutrition played a pivotal role during this intense training phase. After consulting a dietician due to weight management concerns and recognising the need for additional nourishment, I incorporated a protein shake into my diet, particularly on double training days. Meal planning and preparation, alongside strategic nutrition during long runs, were essential for maintaining health and optimising performance. Regular intake of multivitamins complimented my dietary regimen.

A critical component of my preparation was strength training, which ideally would occur twice a week. Given the constraints of my running schedule and personal commitments, I integrated one to two strength sessions weekly. This balanced approach to training, nutrition, and rest was instrumental in preparing me for the challenges of the Comrades Marathon, setting the stage for a formidable but rewarding experience.

## Challenges

My journey to completing my first marathon was fraught with determination and unforeseen challenges. Everything proceeded without issue during the South Coast Marathon until I hit the 25 km mark. It was then that my exercise-induced asthma made a sudden and debilitating appearance. Amidst this struggle, I was fortunate to have the unwavering support of my friend, Mish, who stayed by my side, providing comfort and encouragement as I grappled with my breathing difficulties. Despite the urge to maintain a steady pace, my emotions intertwined with my physical state, leading to difficult breathing that forced me to alternate between walking and jogging for the final 17 km. The experience left me heartbroken and frustrated, yet I crossed the finish line in 3 hours and 55 minutes. Reflecting on this, I chose to focus on the accomplishment of finishing my first marathon despite the setbacks I encountered.

The origins of my exercise-induced asthma trace back to my teenage years, typically triggered when pushing my physical limits or becoming emotionally overwhelmed; the management strategy involved slowing down or stopping altogether, followed by focused breathing to alleviate the symptoms. Although I didn't require an inhaler, the onset of symptoms was a clear signal from my body to reduce my efforts. The condition was not only physically limiting but also a source of immense frustration. The harder I fought against it, the more overpowering it became.

Finding myself confronted by this issue during such a critical race was a harsh reminder of the challenges I thought I had overcome. Despite having qualified for the Comrades Marathon and completing my first marathon, doubts lingered about my body's ability to endure further and improve. The fear of recurring asthmatic episodes loomed large, posing significant questions about my future in long-distance running.

**The Qualifier**

Three months after my initial marathon, I embarked on my second 42.2km race in Pietermaritzburg, targeting a completion time of under 3 hours and 40 minutes to secure a "C batch" seeding for the Comrades Ultra Marathon. The Comrades operates on a batch system based on your marathon qualifying time, with "A batch" for sub-3-hour finishes and subsequent batches classified by incremental time brackets. My training progress showed through faster times and consistent performance. With a robust strategy for the double-lapper marathon, Mish supported me again, conservatively running the first half together. Feeling strong by the 28 km mark, I began to pull ahead. Tracey encouraged me to push for a sub-3-hour 20-minute finish near the final stretch. Calculating the necessary splits, I intensified my pace for the last four kilometres, crossing the finish line in 3 hours, 19 minutes and 1 second, achieving a personal best of over 35 minutes and unexpectedly securing a 9th overall female position. Remarkably, I experienced no asthma symptoms and earned a "B batch" seeding for the Comrades.

Five weeks before the Comrades, a pivotal moment tested my physical and mental preparation. During a routine 20 km run, after stopping to adjust a shoelace, I noticed an inability to lift my left foot properly. Discovering significant swelling on my left shin afterwards, I faced inflammation in my anterior tibialis muscle and tendon—a first for me. I immediately ceased training, recognizing the potential implications for the 90 km race. Frequent applications of ice packs, acupuncture, compression, and leg elevation became my regimen. Four weeks of rest ensued, leaving me hopeful yet uncertain about my race readiness. The swelling subsided in three weeks, but I continued with massages, icing, and needling to ensure complete recovery. A pain-free 5 km run a week before the race offered a glimmer of hope.

Mental resilience is paramount in ultra-running, perhaps even more than physical preparation. While training volume, pace, and terrain are critical, equal, if not greater, emphasis should be placed on race details, gear testing, mental conditioning through adverse training conditions, and envisaging varied race scenarios to enhance adaptability and resilience. This holistic approach, including focused attention on nutrition, targeted strength training, and recovery, is where actual race readiness is forged.

## Raceday

As I prepared for the ultra-distances, my mantra resonated with me:
"Get to the start line uninjured, even if a little undertrained."

## 4 June 2017, Comrades

Anticipation made sleep elusive the night before the race, especially one as monumental as this. With my gear meticulously prepared in advance, I rose quietly, embraced my farewells, and set off with Mish into the predawn stillness, my nerves surfacing as we drove.

A moment of inspiration came as Katy Perry's "*Roar*" played, its lyrics igniting a sense of motivation deeply connected to my first Comrades Ultra experience. The power of a song to fuel one's spirit in moments of doubt is immense.

As the darkness of the early hours enveloped us, alongside thousands of other runners, we positioned ourselves at the starting line in Durban. Accepting and praying for strength, I focused on my race strategy, which included conserving energy by walking the steep inclines early on.

The atmosphere was charged with a blend of nervousness, excitement, and the crispness of a Durban winter morning. Amidst this collective anticipation, the event's iconic musical traditions, including *Shosholoza*, the *National Anthem*, and *Chariots of Fire*, played, culminating in the crowing of a cockerel, signalling the race's imminent start. Mish remained by my side for the initial 60 km until I urged her ahead, choosing to face the remaining distance solo.

Adopting "A" and "B" goals is a strategy I've learned to value. I aimed to secure a Bill Rowan medal by finishing in under 9 hours. However, as fatigue set in around the 60 km mark, I adjusted my approach to focus on completing the race and embracing the experience rather than the stringent time goal.

The journey's final stretch was one of reflection and absorption of the surrounding energy, culminating in a finish time of 9 hours and 19 minutes. The joy of completion was mixed with the physical toll of the race, highlighted by the gruelling post-finish staircase—a stark reminder of the day's exertions.

Crossing that finish line, the immediate challenge was physical and emotional. The post-race obstacles, especially the staircase, presented a final test of resilience, akin to an unspoken rite of passage for every finisher.

Having conquered the Comrades Ultra Marathon, the question lingered: "Now what?" This accomplishment marked the culmination of months of preparation and the beginning of a new chapter in my running journey, filled with reflections, learnings, and the inevitable contemplation of future challenges.

## Second Time Round

Embarking on consecutive Comrades Marathons presents a unique challenge, offering a "back-to-back" medal for those who complete their first two attempts consecutively. My training for the second, a "down" run from Pietermaritzburg to Durban, incorporated lessons from the past with refined goals and aspirations. Despite the "down" descriptor, the route is notoriously undulating, requiring a nuanced strategy.

My preparation was rewarded when I maintained my "B batch" seeding, an achievement confirmed at the Deloitte Marathon. I finished as the 4th lady in 3 hours 15 minutes, a testament to my improved performance and a prelude to the Comrade "down" run. June 10, 2018, marked the date of this endeavour. The familiar cocktail of nerves and doubts accompanied me to the starting line, where I harboured a secret ambition far beyond merely finishing. In shorter trials, I had experimented with pushing my pace beyond conventional wisdom, often with surprising success, despite the physical strain evident to all observers. For this Comrades, I aspired for a Silver medal, necessitating a finish under 7 hours and 30 minutes, a lofty goal kept close to my chest.

The race revealed the limits of my daring. Just past halfway, as my muscles began to cramp and burn, the realisation that my silver ambition might be unattainable set in. Yet, the support of my family in Kloof provided a momentary lift, though the physical toll was undeniable. The walk from Cowies Hill to the finish, over 15 km, was a journey through frustration, disappointment, and mistaken goals. Encouragement from fellow runners corrected my misjudgement of the required finish time, allowing me to adjust my aim to a sub-9-hour finish, which I achieved in 8 hours and 39 minutes. While I fell short of my silver goal, I earned both the Bill Rowan and the back-to-back medal, a bittersweet but valuable lesson in stretching beyond comfort zones.

This experience underscored the dual nature of ambition: the triumphs and the setbacks, each offering its lessons. Victory and defeat are two sides of the same coin, essential for self-discovery and growth. It's not just about physical endurance but also about resilience, the ability to learn from every outcome, and the relentless pursuit of personal bests. Elite athletes embody this resilience, building upon each failure and success alike. Ultimately, perseverance, the capacity to absorb lessons from every situation, forges the path to achieving dreams.

**Two Oceans Ultra-Marathon**

After achieving back-to-back finishes at the Comrades ultra-marathons, I was in peak form and decided to tackle one last ultra—the Two Oceans Ultra Marathon in Cape Town, spanning 56 km. On April 20, 2019, I found myself at the start line, surrounded by the pre-dawn chill and the palpable buzz of runners packed tightly together, all brimming with nervous energy. The ultra runners set off before the half marathon groups, adding to the congestion and excitement. My eyes were on the "5-hour bus," a pace group led by a runner carrying a flag indicating the target finish time. Despite less than ideal-preparation, I aimed to finish within five hours.

The race commenced with the sound of the starting gun, sending us weaving through obstacles like discarded bottles and uneven paving. The initial chaos soon gave way to a steadier rhythm as the crowd thinned and each runner found their stride. However, the day brought unexpected challenges. The organisers had rerouted the course from the scenic Chapman's Peak to Ou Kaapse Weg two days prior due to unforeseen circumstances. While I was familiar with both routes from countless cycling trips, running them presented a new challenge, particularly the significant camber of Ou Kaapse Weg. This slant in the road forced us to run at an angle, complicating my efforts to maintain a steady pace.

As I reached the summit of Ou Kaapse Weg, my pace had already slowed from my initial goal. Still, the encouragement from volunteers and a burst of refreshments reinvigorated my spirits. Resolving to adapt to circumstances, I shifted to plan B—to finish rather than pushing for a sub-5-hour time. The marathon stretched on, each kilometre testing my resolve and adaptability.

Approaching the finish, a surge of energy propelled me forward, spurred by the anticipation of seeing my father at the line. He had made significant efforts to be there, navigating through the crowd and uphill terrain despite his physical difficulties. Crossing the finish line in five hours and eight minutes was both exhilarating and exhausting. I cherished the special medal commemorating the 50th Two Oceans Ultra Marathon. Still, the true highlight was my father's presence, a poignant reminder of the enduring bond and legacy we shared in running. His effort to support me, mirroring his past achievements in this race, underscored this event's deep personal significance, making it an unforgettable chapter in my running career.

# Phase 2: Preparation

**Finding Hope**

**Trail Running**

After the Two Oceans Ultra, I shifted my focus from ultra running to shorter distances and tried something completely new. Despite rigorous training, I was not achieving my targets in road running—I missed breaking 20 minutes for a 5 km by just under 20 seconds, fell short by 3 minutes for a 10 km, and was over three and a half minutes away from my half marathon goal. This mounting frustration was sapping my passion for running, urging me to seek a change before my love for the sport waned further.

The solution came in a vibrant shift to trail running, sparking a renewed passion and vigour within me. I began my trail adventures running through the Westville Eco trails during the early winter mornings, guided by the beam of my head torch and the camaraderie of the local weekly running group. Despite warnings about the risks of twisting an ankle, trail running significantly enhanced my strength, balance, proprioception, and reactive skills. Navigating in the dark became a skill, teaching me the importance of a reliable headlamp—I learned quickly that anything less than 300 lumens would cast too many shadows, increasing the risk of a fall.

My journey led me to join the Trail Snakes group in Hillcrest, a community that gathered every Wednesday and Sunday morning for runs in the upper highway area. The group was led by the charismatic Grant Cummings, who shared his profound passion for trail running and ensured inclusivity within our diverse group. An exceptionally talented runner, Grant would accommodate slower participants by encouraging faster ones to add extra loops so everyone could regroup periodically. His knowledge of the trails and support for local cafes post-run—affectionately calling cappuccinos "slice of chino"—added a social dimension that enriched our experience. His commitment extended beyond running; he actively engaged in community support and charity fundraising, mainly through participation in the Comrades.

Inspired by Grant's example and the inclusive spirit of the trail running community, I initiated a ladies-only trail group, the Wander Women. This group fostered a shared passion for trail adventures among its members and mirrored the inclusive, supportive ethos I admired in the Trail Snakes. More details on this particular group will follow, highlighting how trail running rejuvenated my love for running and led to meaningful community engagement and personal growth.

## Reconnecting with my first passion

After taking a two-year hiatus from hockey, I rejoined the sport in 2019 with St Mary's hockey club. The team, playing in a competitive league, was a harmonious blend of experienced athletes and younger schoolgirls, creating an enriching environment for both age groups. Returning to the hockey pitch was exhilarating, and I balanced this with regular runs during the week, complemented by hockey matches on Sunday afternoons.

My running prowess was notably peaking during this period, coinciding with the cross-country season. On May 18, 2019, I participated in the Burman Bush cross-country race, a challenging two-lap, two-kilometre course. The race began with a jostle of competitors, quickly transitioning to a grassy, undulating stretch that led to a steep descent followed by a significant climb to the route's highest point on a tarred surface. After a swift descent, the second loop commenced. Unaware of my position in the race, I closely followed the woman ahead of me. Noticing her discomfort with the technical aspects of the trail, I seized the opportunity to overtake on the final turn, sprinting to the finish line to secure first place—a triumphant start to the season. This victory fueled my aspiration to represent my province, Kwa-Zulu Natal, in the national cross-country team, a dream sparked by my desire to compete at a higher level in the sport I loved.

The momentum continued into the hockey season. On May 26, 2019, at the St Mary's hockey pitch, we played our third game of the season. The match commenced with our usual warm-up routine, focusing on goal shooting to prepare our goalie and find our rhythm. The game was intensely competitive, with both teams demonstrating skill and determination to maintain possession. I was actively involved, running across the field in my midfield position, when I felt a sharp pull during a series of lunges for the ball in the second half. Something was wrong.

**I collapsed to the ground.**

Though there was no immediate pain, the sensation of something tearing through my body as I lunged was unmistakable. With my background in physiotherapy, my mind raced with possibilities of the injury's severity, though the exact nature was unclear. Despite the lack of pain, I managed to walk off the field, fueled by adrenaline and frustration. In a temper, I threw my hockey stick and muttered some choice words, my emotions boiling over. My teammates, trying to offer support, suggested icing the presumably injured area—my left hamstring—and reassessed whether I could return to the game. However, I knew my participation was over for the day.

As the match concluded, my disappointment and anger culminated in tears, especially after our team's loss. I collected my children, and we headed to the car. It was then that the pain began—a sharp, piercing sensation shooting into my buttock, heralding the start of what would become a constant battle with pain over the following months. The drive home was manageable, but soon after, the neural tightness set in. I found myself unable to sit on my left buttock, and extending my left leg caused excruciating pain that radiated down to my foot. Yet, lying down with my legs slightly bent brought no pain at all.

The disparity in my symptoms was baffling—how could I walk with relative normality yet struggle to perform simple actions like bending over to remove my sock? The uncertainty of the injury's implications loomed large: What exactly had I done to myself? More importantly, the questions that haunted me were whether I could run and play hockey again and how this injury would affect my active lifestyle.

## Rehabilitation

The initial ten days post-injury were marred by severe neural pain. During the first three days, the discomfort was so intense that Glen had to assist me with putting on my shoes, as bending triggered unbearable pain and tightness down my left leg. Despite my expertise as a physiotherapist, self-assessment and further examination by Glen yielded no precise diagnosis. My hamstrings retained their strength and showed no pain upon resistance testing, which was perplexing. The symptoms indicated significant neural tension without the typical signs of nerve damage like pins and needles or numbness. Intriguingly, I could perform actions like hopping on my left foot or kicking a wall without pain, and palpation revealed no specific points of discomfort along the leg. Yet, the struggle and pain were real, plunging me into despair and self-doubt about my professional skills and the future of my running career.

In search of answers, I consulted my biokineticist, who was equally baffled by my condition. We identified three activities I found impossible to perform, which would serve as benchmarks for monitoring my recovery. The first was a left-side plank, which caused pain and was unmanageable for me to hold. This led us to suspect potential issues with my gluteus medius or an acute tendinopathy. The second activity involved lying on my back with both feet elevated on a step, from which I was supposed to lift one leg and press down with the other to raise my buttock off the ground. This movement, aimed at engaging the posterior sling of the hamstring and calf, was beyond my capability; I had no power to execute it, which was shocking and frightening.

The third activity, jumping on a trampoline, which I found similarly challenging, was yet another stark reminder of the severity of my condition. Each failed attempt to perform these movements not only tested my physical limits but also my emotional resilience, leaving me feeling desperate and cornered.

#%&% (Indeed, only a swear word could capture the intensity of my frustration at this juncture).

For the first time, I grasped the severity of my injury when I couldn't lift myself off the floor at all—not even an inch, and not even through pain. The third activity that revealed the extent of the damage involved a mini trampoline. As soon as I jumped onto this unstable surface, I felt an electrifying bolt of pain shoot through my left buttock, lasting for five seconds, followed by a dull ache that persisted for an hour. Oddly enough, I could perform single-leg hops and jumps without pain, which added to my confusion.

I applied ice daily to manage the discomfort, choosing not to take any medication. It felt as though I was sitting on a golf ball at times, so my focus was on managing the swelling and avoiding further irritation to the area.

Despite weekly progress in my strength sessions, mainly concentrating on my legs, I still couldn't perform the initially painful exercises. I would attempt them again every few weeks, only to be met with the same frustrating and depressing outcome. Initially, I avoided any movements that stretched the hamstring tendon, particularly those requiring a flexed hip position. Over time, as the discomfort decreased and the pain eased, I cautiously reintroduced squats and lunges, gradually increasing the intensity.

Six weeks post-injury, I began running again six weeks post-injury, starting with a 3 km walk/run three times a week and building up to five runs per week.

Although I was consistently overtaken at time trial races, limping along at the back with virtually no pace, I was pain-free while running, which motivated me to persist. Despite incorporating speed work and thrice-weekly strength training, I saw no speed improvement. If I pushed too hard, I experienced a dull ache in my left groin/adductor area. It was later explained that this was my adductor compensating for my hamstring, essentially acting as the "fourth" hamstring.

Sitting even for short ten-minute periods still caused discomfort—a dull ache that intensified the longer I sat, deep in my buttocks. The movement provided slight relief, but the ache remained a nagging reminder for hours afterwards. If sitting were unavoidable, I would either stand, lie on my side, or double up on pillows for cushioning, which helped somewhat.

Over four months, I gradually increased my running distance to over 30 km at a time, albeit slowly and without pain. This progress was a mixed blessing—I was elated to run longer distances again but also disheartened by the slow pace. As a competitive person, I found it hard to accept that my running might permanently be slower than before. Although I could run slowly, my drive to race and push my limits was undiminished, leaving me conflicted about my recovery and future in competitive sports.

## Hitting Rock Bottom

Every day, I grappled with the fear that I might never regain my former speed. Although I maintained a stoic exterior, the pain of this realisation cut deep. Joining my running friends, unable to keep pace with them, was a stark reminder of my limitations. I attempted to adjust my mindset but often cried in private, oscillating between self-pity and gratitude for at least being able to run, albeit slowly. This period was incredibly challenging.

Initially, I had to run solo to accommodate my slower pace, which was a lonely experience. Running has always been a social activity for me, where the joy comes from the friendships as much as the exercise. Being isolated from this group strained some friendships but also revealed who my faithful supporters were—those who reached out even when I couldn't keep up. This experience profoundly influenced my approach as a physiotherapist, reinforcing my commitment to helping other runners maintain not only their physical health but also their emotional and social well-being.

As the year progressed, I continued my rehabilitation and worked as a physiotherapist. In September, amidst ongoing personal challenges, I decided to open my own physiotherapy practice, introducing new stresses and responsibilities.

My fragile hope was cruelly dashed on Tuesday, 27 August 2019, during a trail run in the Krantzkloof Conservancy with my friend Kim. Everything was fine until, in the final kilometre, I struck my left leg against a protruding root. The intense pain that shot through my buttock as I fell was agonising, and I couldn't help but scream. This injury was a devastating blow. Despite my diligent adherence to my rehabilitation and training regimen, I was still struggling for speed and now faced another setback. I felt as though I had hit rock bottom, and it was unclear how, or even if, I could find a way back from this low point.

## Now What?

We hobbled back, and I felt utterly shattered. As someone who generally maintains a positive outlook, I found myself sinking into one of the darkest moments of my life, plagued by daunting "what if" questions:

What if I could never run again?
What if I could never run without pain?
Overwhelmed, I sobbed uncontrollably.

In search of answers, I visited Caron, my physiotherapist. I had previously worked for her and greatly respected her straightforward, no-nonsense approach. She conducted a thorough assessment, checking for any irregularities or signs of a detached hamstring, testing my strength and examining other areas. My lumbar region was tight, likely a compensatory response, but no definitive issues were identified. Recognising the extensive efforts I had put into rehabilitation; we decided that an ultrasound scan was necessary to investigate the ongoing pain and dysfunction.

I scheduled the ultrasound for the following week. The wait was agonising, filled with a sense of hopelessness similar to preparing meticulously for a race, only to see it cancelled or having to withdraw due to injury. Despite the despair, I strived to stay focused and practical, awaiting the scan results.

Arriving at the clinic alone felt strange, as I was more accustomed to providing medical care than receiving it. I entered an empty room to change, the chill of the air mirroring the cold uncertainty I felt inside. Despite my background in physiotherapy, I had no clear expectations—perhaps they would find nothing and suggest further tests or more rehabilitation, which I felt had already been exhausted.

The radiologist's manner was formal and concise, providing brief instructions for positioning myself on the examination table. The cold ultrasound gel momentarily distracted me from my anxious thoughts as the scan commenced. It was a quick process, examining my left hamstring and glutes before comparing them to the right side. After the equipment was put away, the radiologist delivered the diagnosis in a monotone voice:

**"Your left hamstring is completely detached by 2 cm."**

I was numb. The reality of the situation settled in, leaving me to confront the full implications of my condition and the long road that lay ahead.

In my 15 years as a physiotherapist, I had never encountered a hamstring detached from the ischial tuberosity—the part of the pelvis. Overwhelmed, I asked the radiologist what this meant for my future. His indifferent shrug and remark that I'd have to live with it, left me wanting to scream. Frustrated and unable to vent through running, which was now impossible, I rushed to my car and burst into tears as soon as I was alone. I sobbed uncontrollably on the phone to my mom, who was initially confused until I managed to explain the situation.

Seeking further guidance, I spoke with Caron, who referred me to a sports orthopaedic doctor, hoping for more valuable answers. My frustration with the medical profession, to which I had dedicated my heart and soul, grew. When I met with the orthopaedic consultant, he reviewed the ultrasound results but echoed the radiologist's advice to live with the injury and continue rehabilitation. Unsatisfied, I pressed him, posing a hypothetical question:

"What if I was an elite athlete in your clinic? Would you still suggest I live with it, or would you recommend surgery?"

He didn't hesitate to answer that surgery would be the course of action for an elite athlete, exposing a double standard in patient care that deeply troubled me. I was trying to understand why the same care and advice weren't readily offered. Determined and equipped with my professional knowledge, I advocated for myself, which led to the surgeon finally proposing surgery as an option. This potential for a different outcome revealed a stark inequality in treatment based on a patient's perceived status, which I found profoundly unjust.

In my practice, I strive to present all patients with every possible option and outcome, enabling them to make informed decisions about their health. This experience underscored the importance of advocacy in medical treatment—everyone deserves the same level of care and information, regardless of their status. The journey to recovery, or possibly beginning anew, highlighted the critical need for equality in medical care and the power of persistent self-advocacy.

Wednesday, 25th September 2019, marked a significant turning point: the day of my operation to reattach my left hamstring to my pelvis using three helicoils. Approaching the surgery, I felt calm and anticipation, buoyed by the hope of restoring my physical capabilities and perhaps even my running speed. Having found a surgeon whose expertise and approach I trusted completely, I felt reassured despite the inherent risks of surgery. My trust wasn't just about his surgical skills but also about his ability to communicate effectively, demonstrate empathy, and understand when to refer to cases beyond his scope—qualities I find essential in any healthcare professional.

Thankfully, the surgery went smoothly. Upon waking, my first action was to check the mobility of my foot, and it was a relief to find that I could move it up and down — confirming the sciatic nerve was unharmed. Noticing the absence of a knee brace, I realised the hamstring length was adequate and wouldn't require restriction, which was another positive sign.

Post-operation, the surgeon provided a debriefing. He had successfully removed a significant amount of scar tissue and reassured me that, apart from potential minor skin numbness on my inner thigh, the outcomes were favourable. The sciatic nerve was intact, and the hamstring was optimally positioned. The recovery protocol was clear: six weeks of non-weight bearing on crutches, a check-up and a gradual three-month rehabilitation process to ease back into walking and daily activities before progressing to more intense exercises.

However, all of the positive news came with a crushing realisation. My days of playing hockey, a sport I deeply loved, were conclusively over.

The risk of re-detaching the hamstring was too high in fast-paced, direction-changing sports like hockey. This was a devastating blow, but I resolved to focus on the possibility of returning to running at full capacity. The prospect of eventually regaining some of my former speed provided a glimmer of hope amidst the challenging rehabilitation journey ahead.

This period of recovery and adjustment wasn't just about overcoming physical barriers but also about adapting to a new lifestyle where fast, competitive sports were no longer a part of my life. As daunting as this reality was, it was a challenge I was prepared to face head-on, armed with my usual optimism and a detailed recovery plan.

## My own physiotherapy practice and healing

In September 2019, I took a significant step: I left my permanent job as a physiotherapist to start my practice. It wasn't a decision I made lightly; I had resisted the change most of the year. However, the work environment had become increasingly toxic, and the daily dread of interacting with disagreeable colleagues made it clear that it was time to move on, even if it meant stepping far outside my comfort zone.

Life teaches us that growth often occurs when we dare to spread our wings and leave the safety of the familiar behind.

I opened my small physiotherapy practice in the heart of Westville, Durban. Just three weeks later, I underwent an operation on my hamstring. The post-surgery recovery was challenging, mainly because I couldn't drive for six weeks and needed to use crutches for the initial four weeks. Despite being a physiotherapist who teaches others to use crutches, which afford freedom and mobility, I found them cumbersome, especially when carrying anything.

## CRASH

One day, while attempting to slide a favourite coffee mug across the countertop to drink in the lounge instead of the kitchen, I watched in horror as it crashed to the floor, scattering shards and coffee everywhere. Cleaning up was a precarious task, but I managed without slipping and could only laugh at the situation—it was one less mug to wash.

Towards the end of my recovery, I persuaded my surgeon to allow me to use just one crutch for the last two weeks and then wean off entirely by the six-week mark. Celebrating the day I could finally be crutch-free was a small but significant victory; I could finally make and carry coffee without countertop acrobatics. During the first few weeks of running my practice, I still needed crutches and became adept at navigating the stairs leading to my office. I used backpacks to carry essentials and relied heavily on my right leg, which grew more substantial from the extra load. I adapted my movements around the treatment table to avoid putting pressure on my left side while treating patients. My personal experience with rehabilitation deepened my empathy and enhanced my connection with my patients, who could see I was not just prescribing recovery methods but living them.

My initial reluctance to start my practice was rooted in self-doubt. I questioned whether I could successfully run a business, attract and retain clients, and grow the practice from scratch. Despite these fears, the unfolding global crisis of COVID-19 soon validated my decision. Not only did the pandemic shake the world, creating unprecedented chaos, but it also confirmed that I wouldn't have been able to continue at my old job due to family commitments.

This realisation brought peace, affirming that the brave choice to start anew had been correct.

**Lockdown**

The last time we gathered socially, without realising it would be our final time for many months, was on March 25th, 2020, for Glen's surprise birthday celebration. His family joined us at our home for a joyful day filled with birthday cake and takeout treats. Little did we know that this would be our last social event before a significant shift in our daily lives. The next day, South Africa was thrust into a nationwide lockdown in response to the rapidly escalating COVID-19 pandemic. This period marked the beginning of a profound era of uncertainty, the likes of which hadn't been experienced in recent memory. Schools, shops, and all forms of public gatherings ceased; our familiar ways of life were abruptly replaced by isolation and the mandatory wearing of masks during the rare occasions we were allowed outside.

I found solace in being with my children during this unsettling time. Owning my own business afforded me the flexibility to adapt quickly. Glen's continued work at the hospital meant we did not face the immediate financial stresses many others were experiencing. With schools closed for three months, we seized the opportunity to spend quality time together, engaging in daily crafts. I kept active with strength training through various online platforms that sprung up to meet the new demands of living apart.

Meanwhile, Glen faced the frontline risks daily. He took stringent precautions, wearing full protective gear at work and meticulously cleaning his clothes and himself upon returning home to minimise our exposure risk, as he was directly treating COVID-19 patients.

The elusive and ever-changing virus forced us all into a mode of constant vigilance with isolation and regular sanitisation as our primary defences. Eventually, as vaccines became available and the virus evolved, presenting new symptoms, the world began cautiously moving towards a new normal. The government implemented a three-hour window during which we could leave our homes for exercise, restricted to a five-kilometre radius and still masked. This small concession was a breath of fresh air, a hint of freedom that rekindled our hopes for a return to normality. Although fraught with challenges, this time also brought unexpected opportunities to reconnect with family, reevaluate our priorities, and adapt to a drastically altered world.

Slowly, signs of a new normal began to emerge. Restaurants reopened, shop hours normalised, and small gatherings became permissible again. We proceeded cautiously, mindful that the virus was still present but seemingly on the decline. For our family, this meant the kids could return to school, albeit under strict new protocols, including desks spaced one metre apart and mandatory mask-wearing throughout the day. I also resumed seeing patients in my practice, adapting to the latest health guidelines to ensure safety for everyone.

The year 2020 became one of unexpected growth and adaptation for our family. We found joy in the increased time spent together at home. The pause in the usual hectic pace of life allowed me to focus entirely on my rehabilitation from surgery without fearing missing out on races, which were all cancelled due to the pandemic. Our daily routines relaxed; we woke naturally without alarms and savoured each other's company without the usual rush to meetings or training sessions. While we missed social interactions with friends and the broader community, this period reinforced the importance of family and simple pleasures like gardening, enjoying mid-day picnics in the sunshine, and indulging in "feasts" where the children loved choosing from an array of food laid out before them.

The adaptability of our children during these times was genuinely inspiring. They demonstrated resilience, adjusting to new routines with a spirit that taught me much about embracing change and finding joy in the journey. However, only some moments were smooth. The children sometimes argued, expressed longing for their friends, and grew weary of the continuous mask-wearing. I, too, felt the strain, missing my friends and feeling the walls of our home close in on us. Yet, I was secretly relieved that there were no running events, as I wouldn't have been ready to compete in them due to my recovery — a lucky reprieve.

Amidst the challenges, there was laughter and light-hearted attempts at joining the latest trends, from baking banana bread to trying out viral exercise challenges like the handstand-shirt-removal stunt, which provided amusement and a welcome distraction. It took several attempts and nearly resulted in a faceplant on the cement, but I eventually succeeded. This mix of fun, challenges, and embracing a slower pace of life marked our journey through a year unlike any other.

Glen indulged my creative ideas for at-home fitness by helping me rig up a makeshift pulley system between the garden swings so I could attempt pull-ups with a band wrapped around my knee. The initial tries nearly sent me flipping over, and it took several attempts before I could manage even a marginal pull-up. This novel exercise setup lasted about a week before it grew tiresome.

A memorable highlight of lockdown was organising our virtual running races in the garden. Fortunately, we had a sizable yard that allowed for a roughly 500-metre track, complete with obstacles and multiple route options—clockwise, anticlockwise, or a freestyle "do-what-you-want-all-over" approach. It was never dull. Each week, I crafted little prizes to keep the excitement alive: the first week's winner received a Strelitzia flower from our garden, the next week, I "won" a basket of luscious home-grown avocados from our enormous tree, and the final prize was a massive delicious monster leaf. I kept track of each loop on a piece of paper, and the kids joined in for a few laps, adding to the fun.

As the year progressed and pandemic restrictions gradually eased, we started seeing the light at the end of the tunnel. Running events slowly resumed, albeit with strict sanitisation and participant limits. The return of these races allowed us to enjoy the company of fellow runners once again. During the lockdown, I managed to maintain some gentle jogging without experiencing any recurrence of sharp pain. However, I remained cautious about sitting on hard surfaces or for extended periods due to lingering discomfort in my buttocks.

With the gradual return to normalcy, I felt ready to set a new ambitious target. I learned about the 13 Peaks Challenge in Cape Town—a non-competitive event perfect for post-lockdown as it had no COVID-19 restrictions and allowed flexible scheduling. Eager to plan this next big adventure, I organised and prepared. But before diving into this new challenge, October brought an opportunity for a family road trip to Pretoria to visit friends. This journey turned out to be more than just a vacation; it marked the beginning of another exciting chapter with the addition of a new four-legged member to our family.

## Storm

I had always dreamed of having a dog as a running companion, although adding another pet was outside our plans since we already had four animals at home. Everything changed during a visit to Mandy Papenfus, where we encountered her new litter of 12 border collie puppies. My knowledge of border collies was limited — I knew they were often referred to as sheepdogs and typically had black and white fur. Glen didn't outright reject the idea when I tentatively suggested adopting one, which surprised me. Upon asking if collies were good running dogs, I was met with laughter and assured that they were one of the most energetic breeds.

That settled it. I was drawn to the tri-colour—black, white, and brown—and there were five puppies to choose from. Mandy recommended a male, which narrowed our choice to one particular puppy: Storm. He was the quietest of the litter, keeping to himself but with gorgeous colouring. He was also the second-largest puppy. Although he was too young to be taken immediately, we arranged for Mandy to bring him to us in Durban a few weeks later. Thus began an exciting new chapter.

A border collie is an exceptional breed, and I continually learn from Storm. He's mischievous, fun, and has turned out to be a fantastic running partner. As I was recovering from my operation and considering that puppies should not run too early to avoid stress on developing growth plates, we both eased into running gradually. By the end of the year, I started training Storm to run with me, which required patience due to his sensitivity to loud noises like trucks and motorbikes, which would either scare him or trigger a chasing response.

Storm's arrival was a delightful addition during the lingering periods of lockdown. With us being home for extended hours, we had ample time to train him. He brought a new dynamic of fun and energy to our household. The joy and enthusiasm he expressed whenever we came home were heartwarming and much-needed during those times.

As restrictions began to ease further, I felt ready to focus on a new goal. This next chapter promised a return to my old pursuits and the beginning of new adventures with Storm by my side.

## A New Goal

"The 13 Peaks Challenge isn't a race; it's about getting out there and exploring our beautiful wilderness areas. It doesn't matter if you hike or run, take two days or months to complete; the most important thing is you have fun doing it." These words by Ryan Sandes, a professional ultra trail runner from Cape Town, encapsulate the spirit of the 13 Peaks Challenge, an adventure he conceived during a trail run with his friend, Kane Reilly. Initially envisioned as a 55 km trail linking various peaks, the challenge quickly expanded into a gruelling 100 km journey with 6,000 metres of vertical climbing. The official route starts at Signal Hill and progresses through a sequence of peaks: Lion's Head, Maclear's Beacon, Grootkop, Judas Peak, Klein LeeuKop, Suther Peak, Chapman's Peak, Noordhoek Peak, Muizenberg Peak, Constantiaberg, Klassenkop, and Devil's Peak, before concluding back at Signal Hill.

As I prepared for the 13 Peaks Challenge, I set several "smaller" goals to build my mental and physical readiness for this daunting endeavour. An African proverb says, "If you want to go fast, go alone; if you want to go far, go together." This wisdom resonated deeply with me and materialised through a newfound friendship with Roxanne Vale, who entered my life towards the end of lockdown.

During this period, I created a five-part trail puzzle challenge to motivate people to return to the local trails, as formal races were still prohibited. Participants would run a designated trail each week and collect a puzzle piece, eventually spelling out "T-R-A-I-L." Roxanne, who committed to completing each segment, collected all her pieces and became one of my closest allies. Our friendship blossomed instantly, with her support proving invaluable as I tackled the Lion500 Open Game challenge.

The Lion500 initiative, founded by Kosta Papageorgiou, encourages participants to ascend Lion's Head 500 times for a cause. Building on this idea, the Lion500 Open Games allowed individuals worldwide to undertake any activity 500 times to support a purpose. Captivated by this concept, I ran 500 km of trails for the Inanda Trail Running Club. Roxanne's encouragement was instrumental as I navigated this extensive commitment, blending the joy of personal achievement with the satisfaction of contributing to a community cause.

Through these experiences, the path to the 13 Peaks Challenge became a test of endurance and a journey enriched by camaraderie, discovery, and a deeper connection to the trails and people who love them.

**Inanda Trail Running Club**
Based in the Inanda Valley, this club is both underprivileged and brimming with talent. The Inanda Trail Running Club desperately needed funds to support their runners and community with daily essentials and running gear.

Embracing this cause, I started recording my trail kilometres for the Lion 500 challenge. This journey would challenge me physically and enable me to contribute meaningfully to this community.

Through my efforts, I raised just over R5,000 for the club. Knowing that these funds would help build and support the trail community financially filled me with immense joy. There's always a wish to do more, to give more, but seeing the direct impact of these efforts was profoundly gratifying.

From October 2020 to January 2021, I ran 500 kilometres of trail, completing my final kilometre at Honey Trails in Inchanga, where I started. Despite the wet and miserable weather that final morning, I was accompanied by a dedicated group of friends. To my surprise, two other extraordinary ladies, Estelle and Renette, were also there, cheering loudly and celebrating with balloons at the finish line. Their presence reminded me of my incredible support system—friends who stand by you through thick and thin, celebrate your achievements unconditionally and surprise you when you least expect it. Over the years, I've realised that the strength of friendships isn't necessarily measured by the quantity of time spent together but rather by the quality of that time. Meaningful conversations, even if infrequent, can forge lasting bonds: the shared experiences, the listening, and the mutual encouragement we give one another cement these relationships.

Roxanne, one of those cherished friends, crafted a beautiful trophy for me to commemorate completing the Lion500 Open Games. It featured a handmade beaded lion perched atop a rock, complete with a plaque. Such gestures of love and support, especially amidst challenging conditions, underscore the importance of friendships. They provide comfort in our darkest moments and serve as a sounding board during struggles and a source of celebration in times of joy.

Indeed, friends also play a crucial role in offering honest feedback and helping us navigate corrections in our paths. Known for my straightforward approach, I often speak my mind, even when it is difficult. Although I may not always be the most eloquent or use the perfect words, my intentions are always rooted in a desire to nurture and mend relationships, even if it means apologising afterwards.

This transparency and commitment to authenticity have shaped many of my most valuable friendships and continue to guide how I interact within my community and beyond.

My training schedule became a well-oiled routine structured around my commitment to running five days a week, with Mondays and Fridays designated rest days. Wednesdays and weekends were perfect for trail runs, while the other days were reserved for road running. Balancing this schedule with the responsibilities of having two young children and a supportive husband often made me reflect on my priorities. I regularly questioned whether pursuing this dream was selfish or worthwhile. I knew I needed to commit fully to prepare and succeed if it was the latter.

My daily routine involved waking up around 4:30 to ensure I could finish my runs by 6 AM. This early start allowed me to manage my time effectively, although it meant being disciplined about my bedtime to ensure enough rest. Weekend mornings started even earlier, allowing me to fit in longer runs and return mid-morning, minimising the impact on family time. Despite the intensity of my peak training, which left me quite exhausted during the day, I managed to stay energised with afternoon naps and focused on solid nutrition for recovery. I also made it a point to go to bed earlier to ensure my body received the rest it needed.

To complement my running, I incorporated strength training specifically targeting my legs, fitting in these sessions once or twice a week for about half an hour. This was crucial not only for enhancing my running performance but also for preventing injuries.

Meanwhile, my physio practice continued running smoothly, with a steady flow of patients daily. I scheduled my appointments to keep my afternoons free, allowing me to pick up my children from school at lunchtime and spend quality time with them in the afternoon. These moments were precious — enjoying the simple joys of life with young children who had no homework yet.

Evenings were a special time in our household. Glen would usually be home just before 5 PM, and we made it a point to have our evening meal together as a family. During these meals, we engaged in seemingly insignificant yet profoundly meaningful conversations—discussing school activities, sharing stories about the latest book someone had read, or simply revelling in the day's excitements. These moments underscored the balance I had strived to achieve between my athletic ambitions and my family life, proving that pursuing personal goals while fostering a nurturing, supportive home environment was possible.

As my training intensified, so did my focus on nutrition, which became a critical component of my daily routine. I heavily relied on smoothies to support the energy demands of my rigorous schedule. These weren't just any smoothies but carefully crafted nutritional powerhouses. I typically used yoghurt as a base, enriching it with nuts, seeds, and carbohydrates.

Common ingredients included oats for their slow-releasing energy, bananas for a quick energy boost and potassium, and berries for their antioxidants. Whey protein powder became a staple in these smoothies, enhancing their flavour and providing the essential proteins needed for muscle recovery and growth. This addition was particularly important post-run, helping to speed up muscle repair and reduce soreness.

Glen took on the role of chef in the evenings, preparing our main meals. While he handled most of the cooking, I often added extra protein sources to meet my nutritional needs. This could be anything from a piece of grilled chicken to a scoop of quinoa or a few extra spoonfuls of lentils.

Fats were another crucial part of my diet, and I leaned heavily on various nut butters. My go-to choice was standard peanut butter and more specialised nut butter, like almond or cashew. These added a delicious creaminess to my smoothies and provided healthy fats, which are essential for long-term energy storage and satiety.

This meticulous attention to diet played a significant role in sustaining my energy levels and overall health, allowing me to meet the physical demands of my training while also managing a busy family life. Proper nutrition was not just about fueling my runs; it was about maintaining balance and ensuring my body received the necessary nutrients to function optimally on and off the trail.

My journey with nutrition took a significant turn when I began training for the Comrades ultra-marathon, a period marked by intense physical demands and high stress. Recognising that my weight was rapidly declining and understanding the potential long-term impact, I sought the expertise of a sports dietician. This decision proved invaluable as it opened my eyes to the intricacies of sports nutrition, particularly the importance of maintaining a balanced diet enriched with proteins and healthy fats, especially during heavy training phases.

The dietician helped me understand the need for a daily balance of nutrients and taught me about the significance of portion sizes. She introduced me to quick, healthy meals that I could prepare easily or in advance, which was crucial for my busy lifestyle. One of the key insights was that the scale only tells part of the story. It's vital to notice how your clothes fit, consider body calliper readings or scans to assess body composition, and understand natural body fluctuations such as those caused by the menstrual cycle, which can significantly affect how one feels and appears due to bloating.

My dietician was initially shocked to learn that while my dinners were balanced, the rest of my daily meals were inadequate, leading to early evening hunger pangs. This was a clear signal from my body that it needed more sustenance throughout the day. By incorporating more proteins and healthy fats into every meal, I eliminated those pangs and noticed a substantial boost in my energy levels.

She emphasised the importance of fueling for the activity level and ensuring proper nourishment during and after physical exertion to optimise muscle recovery and growth. If I didn't adequately fuel my body during or after my workouts, recovery would be slower, and my body might even metabolise muscle tissue for energy. Particularly for runs longer than 15 kilometres or lasting over an hour and a half, it was essential to eat a small snack beforehand and to refuel shortly after finishing.

This holistic approach to nutrition profoundly changed my training regimen and physical well-being, allowing me to meet the physical demands of ultra-marathon training effectively. I learned that to achieve the best possible outcomes and recovery, especially in ultra-running, one must place as much emphasis on nutritional strategy as on physical training.

As I continued to apply these lessons, an unexpected invitation arrived, promising a new adventure and a fresh challenge to use my refined approach to nutrition and training.

## X-Berg Challenge

The opportunity for a new adventure arrived unexpectedly when Pierre Carter reached out to me via Facebook. Surprisingly, I had no prior knowledge of him, nor did he have any apparent reason to know about me. His message was an invitation to participate in the X-Berg Challenge, a race I had never heard of before. Intrigued, I decided to look it up, and what I found piqued my interest immensely.

The X-Berg Challenge is no ordinary race. It's a multi-discipline event set in the breathtaking Drakensberg Mountain range in Kwazulu-Natal, South Africa, pitting runners against cyclists and paragliders. Participants must navigate the course independently, tagging specific points along the way. The challenge can be undertaken solo or in teams, and competitors can choose to stick with one discipline or switch between running, cycling, and paragliding at designated transition points.

Faced with the decision, I opted for the "mini" version of the race—a somewhat less daunting two-day event than the ultra, which spans four days and covers a gruelling 160 kilometres. Despite my initial reservations about attempting such a challenging race solo, I persuaded Roxanne to join me. We were both excited about the prospect and decided to compete as trail runners.

We registered as Team Ojekamanzi, which means "Dragonfly" in isiZulu—a nod to our majestic surroundings in the Drakensberg, often referred to simply as "the Berg." The name was a fitting tribute to the powerful and graceful creatures that inhabit the mountainous landscapes, and it symbolised our hopes of embodying those qualities during the race.

As the event approached, Roxanne and I prepared physically and mentally, ready to navigate the rugged terrain and embrace the unique challenges of the X-Berg Challenge. The anticipation of competing in such a diverse and demanding race added an extra layer of excitement to our training as we looked forward to testing our limits and experiencing the wild beauty of the Drakensberg mountains.

In preparation for the X-Berg Challenge, Roxanne and I decided to spend a weekend in February 2020 to familiarise ourselves with the race terrain, explicitly choosing to scout the middle section of the route. This hands-on reconnaissance mission was crucial given the unique nature of the race, which required adept navigation through potentially unmarked trails.

We dedicated the entire morning to this exercise, spending about 4 to 5 hours on the trails. This part of the course was relatively well-marked, which was a relief. Still, we knew many other race sections featured sparse markings or paths that would abruptly end, leaving competitors to rely solely on their navigation skills. To ensure we wouldn't lose our way during the actual event, we constantly checked our location and stayed vigilant about following the correct direction.

For navigation, I loaded the GPX map route onto my watch, which provides essential guidance. Additionally, we used a comprehensive app on our phones that offered detailed information, including elevation profiles and precise coordinates. Roxanne's familiarity with the area was invaluable; her understanding of the terrain helped us anticipate the general direction we needed to maintain.

Our recce day was bright and beautiful, ideal for spending extended hours outdoors. We came well-prepared with snacks and appropriate gear. One immediate lesson we learned was the importance of wearing long trousers. The trail led us through dense thickets filled with thorns, and we quickly realised why previous racers had recommended protection for the legs. We later discovered that there was a lighthearted award - the grater award - given at the end of the race for the competitor with the most "shredded" legs—a testament to the challenging and untamed nature of the course.

This reconnaissance trip allowed us to test our gear and navigation skills and helped us build confidence in handling the diverse and demanding conditions we would face during the race. It underscored the importance of preparation and familiarity with the course, providing valuable insights that hopefully translate into a successful and enjoyable race experience.

Embarking on ultra trail running was a new frontier for me, pushing the limits of both my physical and mental stamina. These reconnaissance runs provided the perfect opportunity to test my gear, which is critical to ensuring a successful ultra-running experience. The right equipment must not only be comfortable to avoid chafing but also needs to be breathable and reliably waterproof. Learning to pack my hydration vest efficiently was also part of the learning curve. I initially made the mistake of packing essential items too deep inside my pack, quickly realising the importance of having frequently needed gear easily accessible at the top.

Rox and I ran well together, complementing each other's pace and style. Our recce took us up the steep climbs of Bushman's Neck, where we crossed beautiful waterfalls and expansive green mountain ranges. The weather was warm yet mild, creating perfect conditions for our exploration. After a strenuous ascent, we reached the top and proceeded along a gently undulating ridge pathway. These sections were technically runnable, but the long grass made it challenging. While Rox moved effortlessly through the terrain, seeming to float above the obstacles, I became more cautious, feeling cumbersome and constantly watching my feet to avoid tripping. Despite my vigilance, I still experienced a few falls.

As we began our descent, the real challenge presented itself. We needed to navigate through a tricky section filled with thorny underbrush. No matter our direction, we encountered sharp leaves and thorns that ensnared our clothes and gear. The briars clung tenaciously, and we found ourselves battling the terrain and vegetation, which seemed determined to impede our progress.

Eventually, we emerged from the thicket, waist-deep in thorn bushes and found a serene spot by a stream to rest and regroup. We attempted to clear the briars from our gear but soon gave up, choosing to rather sit and refuel. As we caught our breath and enjoyed a brief respite, we were entertained by several playful butterflies dancing around the water's edge, and this moment of tranquillity amidst the challenges served as a reminder of the beauty and unpredictability of trail running, highlighting both the physical and aesthetic rewards of engaging with the natural world.

When I transitioned from road running to trail running, I made a promise to myself: I would always take at least one photograph during each run, even if I was racing. This commitment was born out of a desire to slow down and truly appreciate the stunning surroundings that my feet carried me through. God's creation deserves to be seen and cherished, something that's hard to do when sprinting through trails focused solely on checking splits on my watch. While there's a time for speed and competition, my purpose on the trails is to soak in every moment and marvel at the beauty around me by pausing and taking it all in.

The butterflies we encountered by the stream perfectly embody this philosophy. They only appeared once we sat quietly, their joyful dance a sight. It's a poignant reminder of life itself—we often rush from one task to the next, and our days are a blur of work, errands, and obligations. We eat, shower, sleep, and repeat, rarely stepping off the treadmill of life. We must intentionally slow down to truly appreciate our surroundings and the people we share our lives with. Exploring new paths, waking up early to catch a sunrise, or sharing a conversation with a special friend can enrich our days immeasurably.

Roxanne and I continued our journey after our restful pause by the stream. We soon found ourselves facing a fence with no apparent gate. Our choices were to take a long detour or find a way through. Fortunately, we encountered local sheep herders who pointed us to a hidden gate, saving us hours of extra walking. We remained calm and collected in such situations, carefully considering our options and choosing the best way forward. Without the pressure of time restrictions and with favourable weather, our trek was enjoyable. We chatted effortlessly, discussing everything and nothing as if we had known each other for years.

We documented our adventure, taking photographs—especially jumping shots—and videos to capture the memories. Sometimes, we ran quietly beside each other, absorbing the breathtaking scenery and the magnificence of the Berg. The shared experience was about more than just covering ground; it was about connecting with nature and each other. Spending time together in a meaningful way made our preparation for the X-Berg Challenge all the more special.

Our recce was largely uneventful, though it did teach us an important lesson: we needed "real food" during our runs, not just snacks, bars, and rehydration drinks. We found ourselves quite hungry! As soon as we returned to the house, exhausted, Pierre asked if we wanted to go paragliding with him. Since we arrived, I had been bugging him about paragliding, but the weather was unsuitable. Paragliding requires just the right conditions to be safe. Initially, I asked if we could go the next day, but the forecast looked unfavourable. Roxanne wasn't interested at all, and I was also about to decline. However, I quickly changed my mind, changed my clothes, grabbed a bite to eat, and hiked up a steep mountain with the 10 kg paraglider for what turned out to be an experience of a lifetime.

I'm so glad I did. This was one of those moments where my initial reaction was to say "no." Still, after reconsidering, I realised I didn't want to regret missing out on this opportunity with a highly experienced paraglider. There have been a few times in my life when I've initially declined a great adventure or opportunity, only to rethink and decide to seize the moment. Usually, the hesitation stemmed from laziness or the comfort of routine, but as I've grown older, the phrase "carpe diem" has taken on more significance for me.

This experience reminded me of the importance of pushing past that initial reluctance to embrace new adventures. I often missed opportunities in my younger years because I needed more time to get up or leave the house. Reflecting on those missed chances, I've learned to value spontaneity and the excitement of saying "yes" to life's adventures.

Now I consciously seize the day, embracing the opportunities that come my way and making the most of each moment.

When faced with an opportunity, I always ask myself,

**"Will I regret this more if I say no?"**

This mindset was in full force at the top of the ridge, where Pierre prepared everything for our paragliding adventure. This was his passion, his hobby, and while he was setting up, I took in the breathtaking views around us. We geared up for tandem paragliding, strapped in, and waited for the perfect wind conditions. Pierre explained the takeoff process: when he said "go," we had to run as fast as we could and keep running right off the cliff. Despite the inherent danger, I felt completely at ease, completely trusting Pierre. Once I decide to trust someone, it alleviates all fear and anxiety.

The wind was finally right. We started running, and before I knew it, we were airborne. The silence enveloped us, broken only by the beeping of the altimeter, which indicated whether we were ascending or descending. The beeps grew faster when we descended. It was peaceful and beautiful, and the weather was perfect for flying. While soaring above the mountains, Pierre asked if I got seasick. "Um, yes. What does that have to do with paragliding?"

I soon found out. We needed to catch thermals to gain height, which involved making circular movements in the air. We used the vultures as indicators of where the thermals were. I was amazed at how technical paragliding was; there was so much I didn't know. We continued gliding for another 15 minutes before Pierre said it was time to head back. I started feeling a bit queasy, but it was manageable. Pierre, experienced and unphased, reassured me. His solution for nausea was simple: lean over and let it out if necessary.

As we descended, Pierre asked if I wanted to try a barrel loop (though I didn't need to figure out the exact term). I was excited but warned him that I might get sick. He executed a hard right, then a hard left, holding it so we corkscrewed down rapidly. It was an exhilarating roller coaster feeling. I tried to get sick but was retching since I hadn't eaten much all morning. High up in the sky, the mix of thrill and trust was an indescribable experience.

We landed smoothly in a field, packed away the chute, and then had a 2 km walk back to the house. I felt elated. It was a fantastic life experience and reinforced the importance of saying "yes" to opportunities. The sensation of soaring and the view of the endless Drakensberg mountains from the sky are unforgettable. This adventure reminded me that while such experiences aren't for everyone, the lesson to seize the moment is universal.

The next day, we enjoyed a gentle trail at the base of Monks Cowl, meandering through forest sections with some of the other trail runners. Our group of four maintained a pleasant pace, with Rox leading the way and me running second. As she leapt over a rock, I suddenly heard a whoosh and saw quick movement. Instinctively, I stopped immediately. Right before me was a curled-up puff adder, poised to strike.

This was my first encounter with a snake while trail running. After identifying the snake, I felt immensely grateful for my quick response. The puff adder, known for being the laziest and the fastest-striking snake, has venom that causes muscle atrophy and tissue death. We waited cautiously, and eventually, the enormous snake, well over a metre in length, slithered away.

The encounter brought a rush of thoughts and a stark realisation of what could have happened if I had been bitten, especially being at least 4 kilometres away from any possible help in the middle of the mountain range. It was a sobering moment that left me deeply thankful we both came away unharmed. Life can change in the blink of an eye, reinforcing my commitment to living each moment to its fullest and not hesitating with "what ifs."

After this nerve-wracking encounter, we continued our trail through the forest, ending our journey at a massive waterfall. The day we concluded with a refreshing swim in a Berg river, a perfect way to cap off the adventure. What more could we ask for?

## X-Berg Race Day One

Race day came with a unique set of challenges and strict rules due to the ongoing COVID-19 pandemic. We were grateful that races had resumed, albeit with clear guidelines involving masks, limited participant numbers, and abundant hand sanitisers around the race village. Typically, the X-Berg Challenge takes place in October, but the 2020 event was cancelled, and March became the new race date. We eagerly seized the opportunity to participate. Mask-wearing and maintaining physical distance had become routine, but the beauty of running lay in the vast open spaces of the great outdoors.

Rox and I arrived at registration, buzzing with excitement. We received our well-stocked race goodies and the essential Spot GPS device. As the X-Berg is a self-navigating race, these devices are crucial for monitoring participants throughout the event, adding a layer of safety despite their extra weight. It was beautiful to see new friends we had made, many of whom were tackling the Extreme X-Berg while we were set for the Mini X-Berg.

The weather was calm and moderate, perfect for the race day buzz that filled the air. We enjoyed a meal and prepared for the race briefing. The organisers walked us through the safety measures, emphasising the importance of always carrying our Spot devices, understanding how to activate them, and explaining how the race would proceed. As with most ultra races, there was a strict list of compulsory gear for safety and practicality.

The X-Berg Challenge required participants to tag specific points in a designated order. With three disciplines—trail running, cycling, and paragliding—the challenge was inherently three-dimensional. Gliders had to fly into various zones to tag them before flying out again. The camaraderie among returning contestants felt like a family reunion, with friendships formed over the years rekindled with warm embraces and shared excitement.

Participants could compete individually or in teams of up to four, choosing one discipline or a combination, with specific transition points for switching activities. Rox and I were eager to start, fully prepared for the adventure ahead and the unique experience that awaited us in the Mini X-Berg Challenge.

We began our adventure early on a fresh Saturday morning at El Mirador. The countdown to the start went by in a blur, and before we knew it, we were off. Cyclists surged ahead while runners and paragliders ran side by side. It never ceases to amaze me how efficiently paragliders can run with their heavy packs. Their advantage is evident when they reach a peak and can glide away, provided the weather is perfect.

We started up a gentle hill, and within two kilometres, we shifted to a brisk walk to conserve energy, knowing we had a long journey ahead. As the group began to spread out, we navigated our way forward. Our first tag point required us to push through waist-high brambles, making us grateful for our long tights, which offered some protection from the sharp barbs. We followed contour paths, stopping to take photos and relish each other's company and the breathtaking views.

We constantly checked our GPX route as paths often disappear, necessitating direct navigation. After a few hours, Rox and I found ourselves alone, having decided not to push too hard at the start to enjoy the sights better. However, one tag point proved to be particularly challenging. Despite pre-studying the map, we descended into a deep valley to tag the point, only to realise later that we could have taken a summit route, saving us about three hours.

Just before tackling this hill, I half fell down a slope and twisted my ankle. Fortunately, I could still run, but I had to be cautious with my footing. Although concerned about finishing, I found that the pain was manageable as long as I avoided forcing my foot downwards.

The early challenges of the race, including the twisted ankle and navigation issues, reinforced the importance of adaptability and resilience. Despite the setbacks, we were determined to complete the journey and make the most of the experience.

**X-Berg Race Day Two**

One of the funniest moments of our entire journey happened when we were running along, chatting away, and I encountered a thigh-high grass clump. Thinking it was just loose, thick grass, I charged ahead, only to find a solid rock covered in grass. I collided with it, first bending over at the hips, head and hands to break my fall. Roxanne's initial gasp of disbelief was quickly followed by an echo of laughter through the valley as I called out that I was okay. It must have been a hilarious sight—me with my bum in the air, legs dangling, and arms pinned to the ground, unable to get myself out of the awkward position. Thankfully, Rox was there to share the humour and help me up.

As we neared the end of day one, we faced a significant decision: continue until 11 pm, camping out in the mountains, or head back for a better night's sleep inside from Monks Cowl, stopping around 7 pm. As dusk turned to night, the decision became more obvious. The darkness, creeping cold, and steady rain convinced us to head home. Navigating towards Monks Cowl in the dark, we waited to be picked up. After being on our feet for 12 hours, fatigue set in, and tempers flared, especially since we hadn't packed enough substantial food. Hunger contributed to our irritability.

We made our way to Pierre's home—a short drive away—and spent the night in warmth and comfort, away from the rain. Race rules allowed us to resume from the same point we stopped, so the following day, we intended to start at 5 am but ended up beginning properly around 6 am. Despite the chilly start, it was a beautiful Berg morning. From Monks Cowl, we headed to Blindmans Corner and then to the area we had scouted previously. Familiarity with this section bolstered my confidence despite my legs and body being tired.

The day warmed up, and the skies cleared, revealing paragliders who appeared seemingly out of nowhere. They had taken alternative routes to maximise the favourable weather. Roxanne's competitive spirit kicked in, and we increased our pace, but once the paragliders were in flight, there was no catching them. We continued along the ridge, descended across a stream, and ventured through the woods.

A navigational error led us into a bog, forcing us to backtrack significantly. Despite this detour, we eventually emerged near the road close to the finish. The sight was glorious! With only a few kilometres left, we summoned renewed energy and ran towards the finish line, crossing it with a triumphant "whoop whoop" and a synchronised jump. It was magic.

We were warmly welcomed by the other athletes, feeling a sense of camaraderie and accomplishment. Team Ojekamanzi—Dragonfly team—had an absolute blast. We created lasting memories and embarked on new adventures, with these experiences forever tucked away in our hearts.

## Post-Race and Cape Town Adventure
After completing the X-Berg Challenge, Glen and the kids came to fetch me, and we headed down to Cape Town for a family holiday. This trip was an

excellent opportunity to visit my parents and friends and scout a few more sections of the 13 Peaks Challenge, preparing both mentally and physically for the upcoming adventure.

Ultra running is all about the team. Despite its appearance as a solo sport, it is, in reality, the opposite. During this journey, I met incredible friends who became part of the Peak Peeps, the team supporting the 13 Peaks Challenge. While in Cape Town, we did two reconnaissance runs of areas I hadn't explored before, providing invaluable training and familiarity with the terrain.

Se7en, a fantastic friend with an incredible family of eight kids known as the Hoods, joined me for this part of the adventure. On 26th March, two of the Hoods and I were dropped off at the base of Klein Leeu for our first recce. Despite being teenagers, these boys live and run daily on the mountains and know the routes intimately. They became integral team members for the 13 Peaks Challenge, bringing joy and expertise to the group.

The early morning air was crisp and perfect for our recce. We started our climb from the side of Suikerbossie Road, immediately ascending. The challenge of the 13 Peaks is evident in the name—steep, technical climbs and descents with only a few runnable sections in between. It's essential to have a good idea of what to expect by scouting parts of the route or learning from others' experiences.

Klein Leeu is a peak that demands a lot of scrambling. Both hands are needed to climb, and at one point, you must make a short but brave jump down a section. Being the most scramble-intensive, this peak was a sharp climb but rewarded us with stunning views. From the top, we could see back at the peaks already summited and forward to Suther Peak, the next challenge. I was grateful to have the chance to hike Klein Leeu, as it was more demanding than anticipated and included a lot of effort and scrambling. It's one of the lesser-known peaks, a hidden jewel in the 13 Peaks Challenge.

These recces not only provided excellent training but also built my confidence for the actual challenge. These shared experiences and preparations make ultra-running a team effort despite individual physical exertion. The beauty of the surroundings and the camaraderie with the team made each climb and scramble a memorable part of the journey.

**Recce of Table Mountain and Peaks**
Our second opportunity for a recce took us up Table Mountain to tag Judas and Grootkop Peaks. Early on 30th March, we set off again, embarking on the steep climb up Kasteelpoort to reach the top of Table Mountain. Dropped at the trailhead, we immediately began the ascent, tackling the numerous stairs that led us to breathtaking views. Although the paths are well marked, occasional offshoots can lead you astray, so knowing your route is essential.

Once on top of Table Mountain, we traversed the mostly flat terrain to reach Grootkop. Before summiting this peak, we detoured to Tranquillity Cracks, an apt spot offering incredible views and a serene atmosphere. We then headed towards Judas Peak, following a gently undulating route. Reaching Judas Peak required a significant climb from the base. A convenient cluster of rocks served as stepping stones, enabling us to boost ourselves to the higher rock area. We pulled ourselves up to the primary rock to reach the summit. The scramble was challenging but well worth it for the views and the sense of accomplishment from tagging another peak.

Our descent took us down Llandudno Ravine, a steep, rocky path equipped with a rope and handholds drilled into the rock to aid the descent. After navigating this section, we continued along the contour path to Suikerbossie. Running these routes with knowledgeable friends was invaluable, as they knew the trails well and helped me visualise and mentally prepare for the challenge. Envisioning how I would feel at this stage and keeping track of the mileage we had completed was crucial for my preparation. The mountains were, as always, glorious, especially with the added benefit of little wind and sunny weather.

These reconnaissance runs significantly boosted my confidence, providing a practical understanding of what to expect. However, it was necessary to remember that during the actual challenge, I would have already accumulated significant mileage in my legs before reaching these points. Recceing as much as possible and studying maps gave me a realistic idea of the upcoming challenges. Thinking something is easier can add to the day's difficulty, so I asked many questions about the sections I didn't scout and thoroughly understood the elevations and distances involved.

What I didn't realise then were the other hurdles that awaited me, entirely out of my control. These unforeseen challenges would test my resilience and adaptability in ways I hadn't anticipated.

# Phase 3: Peak

**13 Peaks Challenge (26 May 2021)**

In ultras, like in life, things can change rapidly. We have a choice: adapt, embrace, or fight the change.

There was a significant hurdle to my 13 Peaks Challenge. Initially, this was a dream I planned to accomplish with a friend, but five weeks before our start date, she could no longer participate. I was gutted. How could I even do the 13 peaks? I had trained specifically for this event, and all my focus was on it. The 13 peaks represented more than just a challenge in ultra running; it was a monumental event to prove that I had recovered and grown even stronger after my hamstring operation. I needed these goals to help me show up daily and dream more significantly than I could imagine. I'd even secured some sponsors and was raising funds for Fit4Rhino.

Feeling disappointed, angry, and at a loss, I wondered how I could turn this around to do it still. I was already praying and hoping that my running and strength training was sufficient, as this was a huge undertaking and a new distance for me. I needed to trust the process, as I had often told my patients. I needed a plan. Doing it solo was not an option—I'd get thoroughly lost and wouldn't enjoy it nearly as much without company.

Then, a miracle happened. I am in awe of how God has everything in place.

Shortly after receiving the disappointing news, I chatted with my friend, Se7en, and she mentioned that her two hoods—who had accompanied me on recces—would be keen to join in. That settled it. A new team was forming, and soon we had both boys, Nuno (whom I had met via my coach at the time-based in Joburg) and Ernest from Cape Town, who I had met through my Lion500 journey. It all came together. We had a great team—Peak Peeps—with three people who knew the route well and the best support crew in Se7en and her husband, which is vital for success.

This new team brought fresh enthusiasm and energy, making me even more excited for the challenge ahead. Together, we would conquer the 13 peaks, proving that anything is possible with the right people and determination.

We oversaw the weather with the new team dynamic and set a starting date and time. Two of us flew around the country to meet the three living in the Cape area. Mid-week would be ideal, as it would be quieter, especially with fewer tourists. We chose Wednesday, 26th May, at noon, when the cannon goes off.

Starting at midday felt unusual. We usually slept the night before and spent the morning doing last-minute packing and preparation. We met at Signal Hill an hour before the start, with family and friends joining us to wish us well. Time flew by, and before we knew it, the cannon sounded, and we were off towards Lion's Head. Signal Hill offers panoramic views of Cape Town and sits beside Lion's Head and Table Mountain. The weather was perfect—moderate temperatures with no wind or rain.

We started quickly, with me yelling at the crew to slow down, reminding them this was just the beginning of a long journey. We descended on the trails towards the road leading to Lion's Head, enjoying the lovely downhill stretch. There was laughter, chatter, and excitement all around. As we began the climb towards our first peak, Lion's Head, we slowed to a fast hike. For me, it was necessary to be conservative at the start; we could always pick up the pace later. Most of us had never done this kind of distance or elevation in one go, which would be brutal. I like planning and making things accessible, especially in ultra running, rather than going full throttle and struggling.

We summited Lion's Head. The views were spectacular, overlooking Cape Town, the harbour, and the glistening sea. Quite a few people were at the summit, but it was less crowded than usual. The climb up to the peak was moderate, and there was a large area at the top to walk around and take in the scenery. It's an ideal spot for sunrises, and many people come early to sit quietly and witness the beauty of a new day from the peak. Peak one, tagged. We made our way down and around the road towards Kloof Corner, which involved a steep uphill climb.

I began eating to keep my energy reserves full, setting my watch to beep every hour to remind me to eat and drink, regardless of how I felt. Nutrition is vital for all training, but especially for ultra-endurance events. As we transitioned from the road up to Kloof Corner, we tackled a steep, short trail section with hands on knees. Our seconders welcomed us at Kloof Corner, where we fuelled up for the long section over Table Mountain, tagging three more peaks—Maclear's Beacon, Grootkop, and Judas Peak—before descending the steep, technical Llundudno Ravine to Suikerbossie, where we reunited with our seconders in the dark.

We climbed above Kloof Corner, winding our way to the contour path towards Platteklip. Platteklip, Afrikaans for "flat stone," lives up to its name with its relentless, step-heavy path to the summit of Table Mountain. It burns the legs early on in this challenge. Fortunately, we were familiar with this route; we all had done it before, so we took our time and slowly made our way to the summit. The chatter and laughter continued as we were still fresh; it was light, and everything was going according to plan. We made a point to always gaze behind us—often, the most beautiful views are behind you, especially when climbing a mountain. It was still mid-afternoon, and we revelled in the beauty of the Cape.

We reached the top and took a short break for food and photos. Then, at a gentle jog, we crossed Table Mountain to bag our second peak, Maclear's Beacon. Although there are several different trails, this section is relatively well-marked, so knowing which one leads to your destination is essential. The terrain is runnable and mostly gentle, with undulating flats. It's easy underfoot, but if it has rained, the footbridges can be lethally slippery.

Soon, the enormous cairn of stones marking Maclear's Beacon appeared. We clambered up to touch the trig beacon, tagging our second peak. We stayed short, wanting to get off Table Mountain before dark. Making our way down and across Table Mountain, we followed well-worn paths, but there are several, so it's crucial to have a great guide or know which path to take. Signs occasionally direct you or indicate where you've come from, but they're not reliable.

The next peak, Grootkop, was easy to run towards, but be aware you can easily miss the "entrance" to it. Suddenly, a small, often overgrown path appears on your right, leading in a snake-like fashion to Grootkop. This peak can be seen, but optimising the best path requires knowledge of the area. The growth is knee-high or higher, depending on the time of year, but a steady path leads you to the coveted next peak trig beacon. As we wound our way around, we spotted the beacon, tagged it, and sat down for a much-needed rest and sustenance.

We narrowly averted disaster! While tagging the peak, one team member accidentally pushed the cairn it was resting on, causing a massive rock to fall inches from my foot! It could have resulted in a severe injury, so I was thankful for my quick reflexes. We had snacks and drinks, and we added an extra layer as the sun began to set. Then, we made our way across to Judas Peak.

From Grootkop to Judas Peak, the run across the top of Table Mountain is gentle. Judas Peak is the easiest to forget and miss. When Se7en did her 13 Peaks Challenge, she ascended the mountain, tagged Maclear and Grootkop, then descended, only to realise later that they still had to tag Judas, requiring another trip. There's no easy way up and down Table Mountain.

A small trail juts out to the left as you run along the path. If you continued straight, which is the main path, you'd head towards Llandudno and off the mountain. Instead, take the left. A short distance up, and you've summited Judas Peak. This peak requires some climbing skills and willing team members. Some rocks are placed beneath to use as a step, as it's a massive boulder you need to clamber onto to reach the trig beacon. Judas Peak is often the easiest to forget to tag despite its difficulty.

Retracing our steps, we re-joined the main path and switched into night mode with our headlamps on. Fortunately, We had the most beautiful evening, with a full moon, clear skies, and calm air. We descended the steep and technical Llandudno Ravine. There's a small section with handholds drilled into the stone and a piece of rope to use, as it's a sizable smooth rock face you need to traverse. After this section, you continue on a contour path. It's essential to know your way when stepping off this path. I almost continued on the wrong path but was reminded to take the more established route to the right. The direction I was heading would have resulted in scrambling and sliding down loose stones, which could have been even worse, especially at night.

We made our way off Table Mountain and met up with our seconders. This was a slightly longer stop to ensure batteries were charged, bodies were refuelled, and any clothing was changed for the cooler evening. I discovered watermelon! Nuno had brought some, and this fresh, juicy fruit hit the spot perfectly.

We jogged along the road, making our way to Kalk Bay, over dunes and then starting the sandy ascent up Suther Peak, fondly known as Suffer Peak. The initial climb was moderately steep and sandy underfoot. The sand gave way to steeper terrain with a narrow path between the bush, eventually leading to more enormous rocks marking the top of the peak. The stars twinkled, and it was the most calm, clear Cape Town evening. The city lights shone brightly, with oversized silhouettes of darkness where the rest of the Cape were asleep. We had a full moon, and it was still, calm, and just the right temperature.

I had taken one water bottle with me to the top, knowing we would replenish our supplies after summiting Suther. Our packs were light, and the only sounds were our feet on the sandy, stony paths and gentle chatter as we continued our first evening together. A headlamp lit up a beautiful little onlooker – a chameleon sitting serenely on a plant just to the side our path. Gentle chirrups of night creatures and the occasional call of a night bird could be heard. It was sublime. I felt utterly at peace, enjoying the quiet company of my companions.

Strangely, as you arrive at the last rock before summiting, you find a ladder resting gently beside it. The ladder was on the wrong rock for the trig beacon when I arrived. I started to climb up only to realise it didn't look like the peak. After switching it to the correct side, we climbed the small ladder and tagged our sixth peak. After a team photo, we clambered down and retraced our steps to the base of Suther Peak and into the arms of our seconders with some more friendly faces! My brother, Brett, and Liezl - my friend - had come out just before midnight after following our progress to meet us.

After a silly sibling dance with Brett and stuffing our faces, Liezl joined us for the 8km upward road to Chapman's Peak. What a pleasant distraction when new friends join you on the journey. We chattered away and made excellent progress. The adrenaline was still pumping, and despite the late hour—after midnight—we reached the base of Chapman's Peak.

When I woke up on the morning of our challenge, I had the frustrating visit of my monthly period. I had wondered why I'd felt so bloated and a little off recently. I get a tad bit moody and crave chocolate a few days before my period. I had prepared for this but needed to change, and no toilets were available. It was pitch black, so I used the darkness before we ascended Chapman's Peak. I am thankful that I didn't experience many difficulties with my period. Occasionally, I have a low, dull ache in my back and feel fatigued leading up to it, but once it starts, it is a steady flow and easy to manage.

The joys of being a woman mean we need to plan for these extra activities in our lives. Early on, I discovered that having my period did not need to deter me from my sport. It's all about finding what works for you. I am grateful that mine are pretty easy to manage with few symptoms, and my heart goes out to women who train hard and struggle if the timing of their period is not ideal for their competition. At one stage, I planned my period to come at the best time when I was training for my first Comrades marathon by using the pill. Looking back and reading up on this debatable topic, I don't think I would do that again. It can add extra pressure to an already complex challenge.

Despite the inconvenience, I felt ready to take on the ascent of Chapman's Peak. It's all part of the journey, and managing these moments with resilience and a bit of humour helps keep things in perspective.

Chapman's Peak was a blur. We had all re-energised with our seconders, changed some clothes, and had our headlamps firmly in place. Mine went out, and I realised it did not last nearly as long as I had thought. What a learning curve. Thankfully, one of the team members had a second headlamp I could use, and we could even use it sparingly, as the moon was so bright that it lit our way.

Chapman's Peak is a steady, moderate climb. I recall much singing and merriment as we hiked up to the top and tagged the Peak, and then some of the team decided it was a good time to run down. I have no problem running in the dark and have trained for it, too. It is an important skill to practise, especially if you take on challenges in the night or early morning darkness. I was just being cautious, as I realised we still had a long way to go as our watches ticked over the 50 km mark—halfway.

From Chapman's Peak, I was unfamiliar with the route and was surprised at how long the next section took us. It was an easy climb up, but it seemed to go on forever. I remember turning to my team and asking how much further, reminding myself of when my kids ask me the same question on long journeys. This section did drag. It wasn't arduous, just lengthy and unexpected in my mind. I'm sure this long trudge, together with it being the early morning hours and knowing it would be a long time until we saw our seconders again, added to the plodding mood I found myself in.

We managed to reach what I thought was the top, yet again, we turned and continued upwards, this time on a firm dirt road until we summited Noordhoek Peak. I am told that the views from this Peak are beyond spectacular. We were welcomed with twinkling stars and a cool breeze, so this peak will need to be revisited to enjoy the views. We took a quick photo in the dark and walked down the long winding road towards Silvermine and our seconders.

We took full advantage of this section and got into good strides as we made our way down steadily to the base. It was easy running on the dirt road, which suddenly opened to the Silvermine section and the top of Ou Kaapse Weg. We crossed over and were welcomed with open arms by our seconders. The cheering and happy voices at this early hour made a difference to our journey. The boys started feeling the miles in their legs and the creeping tiredness.

Muizenberg Peak is an annoying dog-leg to tag, involving an out-and-back route. It is relatively flat until you reach the Peak, which requires only a short, moderately steep climb before you tag it. We were all starting to feel tired and fatigue, and despite this being a very runnable section, we walked the whole way out and back to conserve energy for the second half of our challenge. This is another peak I hope to revisit, as it has magnificent views.

We were silent. A night bird sang, a bat swooped, and the creak of our shoes on the dust was the only other sound. We were all deep in our thoughts, struggling to motivate ourselves. This is where having the most impressive and dedicated crew with you makes all the difference. As soon as they saw our bobbing headlamps, they shouted out with glee and welcomed us back.

We felt rejuvenated from their energy, and two more friends joined the group at five in the morning, bringing the most delicious gift—Krispy Kreme doughnuts! Never has a doughnut tasted sweeter or better than that time on the side road in Silvermine. The group revived, repacked snacks, and fuelled up for the next long and steep section of our challenge.

We crossed the road and began our ascent up a long dirt road to Constantiaberg. The crisp morning air was refreshing against our skin, and the added company sparked renewed chatter in the group. Our trekking poles were out, helping us up the road, and the time flew as we talked away the early sunrise. Marlu and Mitch were the most encouraging company to join us in our next section. From Constantiaberg, we would go down to Constantia Nek, where they would say their farewells.

Our group had slowly drifted apart, each person making their own pace to tag our next Peak. We met up at Constantiaberg Peak, took our group picture, and then made our way steadily down a long, very runnable road.

The only problem now was that some of our group were starting to struggle, and I would go at the slowest person's pace. Two of our group went ahead, and I stayed with the boys near the back as we slowly descended. They looked like they were sleepwalking. The sparkle in their eyes had faded, the earlier chatter in the day had ceased, and they were continuing with one foot in front of the other—which was vital as they were carrying on!

After the road, there is a nasty little hill, followed by a steep, technical section down to Constantia Nek, which seems to go on forever. I was thankful to have my poles helping me on the downhill as my left hamstring was starting to feel the strain. We popped out at the bottom to yet another wonderful welcome, where Nikki had been patiently waiting for us with our seconders at Constantia Nek.

The weather was starting to turn, and we heard that the rain was coming. The boys made their way to their mum, and within a few minutes, they had transformed. They were renewed, lively, bubbling with joy. What had happened? One word: caffeine. We took our time enjoying refreshments and the chatter, then put on our waterproof jackets and prepared ourselves for the worst.

The bizarre part of all this was that the sun was shining at Constantia Nek, there was no wind, and it was pleasant. This challenge taught me that when you go up to the peaks, you can encounter entirely different weather conditions compared to the base, and you need to mentally and physically prepare yourself for both changes. I was starting to feel tired from the journey but thought I had plenty of energy left for the remainder of our trip. My body was doing well, with no real aches or pains except for a slight tightness in my left hamstring. The poles helped with this feeling, especially on the downhill sections.

**Klassenkop**

What a climb. Enough said. In true Cape Town style, the weather changed in a heartbeat. The more we climbed, the worse the wind and rain pounded us. We had already anticipated a turn in the weather, and all had the appropriate gear, but this made it less manageable. Thankfully, the team knew exactly where to go, and we slowly made our way up the paved path onto the long rocky stretch until we came across a deep gully and a tree traversing it. Past the tree was the trig marking Klassenkop peak. We scrambled, took the picture, and carefully returned across the rocky section. This is also one of the most beautiful viewpoints. I have made a mental note to hike up to this Peak on the next sunny day I visit Cape Town to immerse myself in the renowned beauty and to replace the memory of this challenging ascent.

Technically, at this stage in the 13 Peaks Challenge, you are almost done, as Klassenkop is peak 12 of 13. This is where the real challenge comes in. Firstly, the peaks aren't evenly spaced out, so when you are at peak seven and think you are halfway, you are not. The last few peaks are further apart, and when you are most tired, you must mentally break down each section despite being unable to tick off a peak as efficiently. We had Devil's Peak, the 13th Peak, to tag, but first, we needed to descend Nursery Ravine in the rain and wind. This section is treacherous, tricky, and technical at the best of times. I was very thankful for my poles as they relieved the ever-growing tightness in my left hamstring and provided much-needed support.

At this stage, our team had split, with Ernest and Nuno going ahead, and I stayed with the two boys. We rested at the bottom, where Nursery Ravine joins the Newlands contour path. We had all perked up since Constantia Nek, and the weather improved yet again as we descended. We made the most of it and sat for a few minutes, munching at some delicious treats to restore our energy and spirits. It was hard to believe we would complete this challenge, but we knew it was well within our reach despite the climb we had yet to accomplish. We hiked along the contour path, which is undulating and has plenty of steps. When I think of a contour path – which runs along the side of a mountain – my thoughts are often of a nice, gentle path. The Newland contour path has most definitely changed my definition of how I see a contour path. It is steep and climbs a lot. You also need to know where you are going, as there are subtle, small paths shooting off the main path, and unless you know the route, it is easy to take the incorrect one, and then you need to backtrack. The path itself is easy underfoot for the most part. There are small sections where you have to boulder hop over large rocks and pass a gently flowing waterfall at one section, too. I was so grateful that the boys knew exactly where we were going.

Eventually, we reached the base of the turning point to head up to Devil's Peak. We wondered if the other two had gone ahead, but we decided to rest briefly, mentally preparing ourselves before the last big climb to our final Peak. Shortly after we arrived, we were surprised by Nuno and Ernest appearing out of the woods. They had gone at least 30 minutes ahead of us, and we learned that they had mistakenly taken one of the obscure paths and, once they realised, had to backtrack. Reunited again, we slowly walked up the path towards

Devil's Peak. The first climb is to the saddle, then a tiny traverse, the second climb is up to a false peak and, finally, to Devil's Peak. I was prepared for this – or so I thought.

We climbed and finally reached the saddle. We then traversed the next section, which was relatively flat, and the weather turned windier, rainier, and colder. As we reached the base of Devil's Peak, we were met with the most fantastic sight. My heart jumped for joy as the boys' father and siblings hiked up to meet us at that point with chocolate, hugs, and energy. It was a complete surprise to me that they would willingly come up in this horrible weather to summit the last Peak with us. I couldn't believe it. The most amazing part was that the boys were utterly unsurprised as this was normal for them – the family always had each others' backs! It blew me away. I received the biggest hug and laughed so hard.

We didn't stop; we wanted to tag the Peak and descend as quickly as possible to escape this foul weather. Upwards, we trudged. I could not see the path but completely trusted my companions to guide us safely to the top. They knew these mountains so well. When we were unknowingly halfway up, I made the mistake of turning to one of the boys and asking how much further we had to go to the summit. He replied that it was the same distance we had travelled from the saddle to the base of Devil's Peak.

**I burst into tears.**

He was being honest – which is what I wanted to hear – but I still couldn't believe we had so much further to go in this weather. Despite being so close to our goal, I felt defeated. He turned towards me and gave me the biggest hug. I knew I could carry on. In times like these, I am continually reminded of what being in a team and supported means. When we feel we can no longer continue, it sometimes takes that small gesture – a hug, smile, or kind word – and the power that comes with it is incredible. Finally, the trig beacon suddenly appeared in the mist. We quickly tagged it, took a photo, and descended as quickly as we dared in the wet, steep terrain. As we came off the mountain, there was a long section of switchbacks. As the mist and rain slowly subsided, we heard these glorious voices from far below. It was Se7en, her family, my brother, and Nikki. They had come on the Kloof Nek road to welcome us in our final 8 km road run to Signal Hill to complete our 13 peaks challenge.

We had two cars follow us safely along the road. It was dark around six thirty in the evening, but we were on fire: no rain or wind and perfect running weather. We mostly ran this section as it was a great road with a gradual incline at first and then became steeper as we neared Signal Hill. We heard it before we saw it. The beauty of a trumpet playing welcomes us home to complete our 13-peak challenge in 32 hours. One of Se7en's sons had come from afar to play his trumpet and welcome us home. This was a special moment and one I will never forget with a small group of friends who are like family, cheering us in to touch the final trig beacon, which we had left 32 hours before, from being exhausted one moment to being full of fire and energy the next. The taste of completion and accomplishment – knowing that all my training and planning had come to this was gratifying. Hugs all around, and to top it off, Se7en had organised to get us our 13 peak badges ahead of time, and she presented them to us. A special moment indeed. Driving home, I felt refuelled, not tired, and incredibly hungry. When I arrived at my parents' house, it was just before 9 pm. I briefly told them about the adventure and then went to the fridge, snacking on a few tasty food items. Not having slept for ages, I thought I would crash into bed, but – and I've found this often happens – after a shower, I went into bed bodily tired, but my mind would not rest. It took ages for me to fall asleep, and I woke up from hunger at night! After eating some leftovers, I returned to bed and fell asleep again.

The support from friends and family on the route to the WhatsApp group that had been following our movements while Se7en updated them on how we got along. Knowing that people are cheering for you and on your side makes such a difference, and you want to have every little bit of encouragement and support you can muster when you take on these significant challenges. Never underestimate the power of believing in yourself, knowing that at times it will be challenging, but that through training and careful planning, you are resilient and will pass through those hard times by taking that next step until finally, you reach the finish line. Little did I know that one of my dormant dreams would come true.

## An Unexpected Gold

As the dust settled after accomplishing the 13 Peaks Challenge and still living on a high, my focus turned towards my Ultra Trail Cape Town (UTCT) 65 km race at the end of November. I was thrilled that my body had pushed through over 32 hours, 110 km, with 6000 metres of elevation on steep terrain at a slow but steady pace. My hamstring had only got slightly tired from around 60 km in, and with the use of the poles, it was manageable and nothing that I wouldn't expect after doing that kind of distance. I recovered well and soon got back into my weekly routine of five runs with some strength training.

My aim for the UTCT race was different. I wanted to race it. I wanted to do my best and see how well I could do while focusing on having fun. I entered this race in 2019 but withdrew due to my hamstring operation. I had heard so much about these trail events and desperately wanted to be part of them. In 2020, there were no races due to the Covid pandemic, so 2021 was going to be my year. It was enough time after my operation that I felt I could give it a good go – two years. With the correct training and focus I wanted to prove to myself that my body would do well.

Leading up to this race, I made sure that I trained specifically. The UTCT races all have substantial elevation per kilometre, and although I had completed the 13 Peaks on those same mountains and trained the mileage, I needed to include hill training as one of the focus points. The difficulty training for ultras is training for ultras. Only a few ladies in the area are ultra runners; if I do find them, they need to be training for the same races as me. There are some men, but schedules need to align and pace with everyone, and it can become tricky organising training with home, work, and just life!

The beauty of 2021 was to see the opening of races once again. Initially, there were stringent conditions, such as sanitising, wearing face masks, congregating in crowds, and the number of entrants allowed. Still, it was a step forward in healing and seeing some movement towards a new norm after the pandemic.

In between my mileage training, cross-country came onto my radar. I've always enjoyed cross country and desperately tried to make the KwaZulu Natal team, but unfortunately, I narrowly missed out. Despite distance training, I was doing regular speed work – which I believe is vital for running, pushing your speed and mind to keep up and the many benefits of speed training. I had run a few local cross-country races and had done well, so on the 14th of August, I lined up for the provincial trials in the 35 – 39-year-old category. It is a two-lap course of two kilometres and was held at Amanzimtoti Running Club—a beautiful, gently undulating course with plenty of space for supporters. I was nervous but had nothing to lose and would give it my best shot. The gun went off, and we shot out of the starting line.

I kept an even pace for both rounds and gritted my way to the finish, not knowing where I had finished. My club mates welcomed me into the finish, and after I caught my breath, thrilled at how I could run, I found out that I had placed third in my age group and received a bronze medal! I could hardly believe it. After some intense research – asking all my cross-country running friends – I found out that I would most likely make the team race in the nationals, also held in KZN on the same grounds this year. I didn't want to believe it until I was notified. I had hope, but I so badly wanted this that I would not believe it until I saw it. Later that week, I saw my name in print as part of the 35-year KZN cross-country team! I made it. I was going to represent my province and wear provincial colours. This was a dream come true since my hockey days – which sadly would never happen - but I now had this opportunity in cross country.

The national race took place on Saturday, the 18th of September 2021, at Amanzimtoti (or Toti as we call it for short). The day was exciting, and I checked and rechecked all my gear. Masks were still being worn, and you were called to specific warm-up areas after registering. I met up with my fellow teammates. There were four of us in each age group team. We had a strong team and had a good chance of getting on the podium. The day was a perfect running day, and we were one of the first groups to set off in the morning, for which I was thankful. The rain threatened, but we dodged the weather and got to have perfect conditions. We hustled into our pens and lined up. The gun went off, and we shot forward. I kept telling myself not to burn out too soon, but didn't want to be left behind.

Everyone raced so hard! I gave it my all and encouraged one of my teammates struggling with her hamstring on the home stretch as she completed our team. She bravely fought the pain and pushed through to finish. We brought home team gold for the ladies 35 – 39 age group. What an absolute thrill. Not only did I receive an individual bronze medal for the provincial race, but the cherry on top was a gold medal for the national team. A dream came true. I was proud to wear my black and white tracksuit and KZN kit. Always hold on and work for your dreams. You never know how things may turn out; sometimes, they may look slightly different than we anticipate, and that's ok. This dream came true a few years later, but when I was in it, I realised how important it was and that I hadn't let go of it yet and wanted to fight for it. The medal says it all! Never give up. This same "vasbyt" (Afrikaans for pushing oneself to the limit) was used in my training for my next big event.

### 1000 Hills Parkrun Ultra

I needed to do a long run leading up to my 65 km race - at least 50 km with a lot of vert (elevation) to mimic the race. There are a lot of trails around where I live, but the longer ones are flat. Unless I wanted to travel for a few hours and find someone to run with me, I would struggle to get the 50 km with the necessary elevation. I came up with a plan. Ultra running is so much more than just physical training. It is vital to train the mind in the best possible way. Part of this is the discipline of consistently showing up for our sessions, but another aspect is making it mentally challenging. One way to do this is to run loops where, each time, you have the choice to stop, but you choose to keep going and finish the training session.

This was my clever idea to get my ultra training run in with elevation safely and close to home without spending too much time travelling. I ran the notorious 1000 Hills Parkrun ten times – alternating directions each time. This parkrun is known as one of the hardest in the world, with over 200m elevation each lap of 5 km. It is close to home, has parking, and is a safe place to run solo. This was also necessary to test out gear and nutrition, of which I made the most.

How do I make this run more manageable and fun? I invited anyone who wanted to run with me and finish a loop. My kids also made numbers 1 – 10 on pieces of paper so that after each loop, I took a photo of the number of loops we had just finished with the runners who had joined me in that loop. It was amazing. One friend, Chris, ran 40 km as he was also training for the same race, and others joined me for one or two loops. I always had someone with me, which made it more fun, and seeing the numbers progress was motivating. This was a key training session for my race, and not only did it train me physically but also mentally, knowing that I had run ten loops on this challenging course. I knew I had done well.

The course is highly undulating, and reversing it made it a different run. Initially, there is a gentle downhill that continues down into a valley. Often, cows are seen grazing at the bottom. Then, you meander through a tree-covered area with a stream, and the climbing begins after 1 km. There is a particularly steep section – on the average route direction – that we struggled to get up as it had been raining and was particularly muddy. Coming down in the reverse direction, we ended up sliding down on our butts at one point as it was safer and quicker. For 3 km, it climbs up mostly, with a rewarding final kilometre of a glorious switchback down section, which I loved and ran hard. The views are just stunning. Looking out on part of the 1000 hills, you get an idea of the beauty seen with the rolling hills, greenery, and the sheer solitude it offers. Underfoot – apart from the muddy section – it was a packed path that was not too technical or rocky. It is a lovely single track with a clear path and kilometre markings. We took plenty of pictures during the run – we could not ignore its beauty and needed to capture the memories.

My body was well prepared, and I was so grateful for how I found this hard training session. I was not racing it but just getting time on my legs and climbing, and I felt good the whole way through. I had made up my mind to do it, so at no point did I feel the need to cut it short. Having friends join me helped keep me accountable, which is essential. I was being coached then and knew I had my coach to report back to. Depending on your work, it is necessary to have this accountability system, either with friends or a coach or by using a diary or an app like Strava to monitor your consistency. I had also put this run out on social media, and because of its nature – it was a pretty crazy run for those who have done even one lap of this park run – I had committed to it. Find what works for you. My car was stacked with all my nutrition, and my bag was full as though it was race day. I was simulating the day in what I wore, the climbing level, and some distance.

I finished with a jump at 50.18 km after 7 hours and 54 minutes, completing 2228 metres of climbing. I was prepared for the UTCT 65 km in a month.

**Wander Women**

Amid my training, I also grew my small physiotherapy practice. It ticked along during the week, allowing me to fetch my children at lunchtime and do my training early in the mornings. However, I felt the need for more. I had talked with a good friend, Carey, about creating a running group for ladies a while ago. I was inspired by how similar groups in Cape Town had produced wonderful, welcoming communities. With some available time, I decided to start something similar to build a community in the upper highway area, providing a safe place for ladies of all running abilities to run and explore the beautiful trails we had on offer.

Thus, Wander Women was born. I needed to make the group sustainable for me to organise, and the best time for me was Tuesday mornings. Since many were already in the area, I didn't want to have another early morning group. This would be a unique group, being for ladies only. The idea was to create a safe space where women could come without feeling judged or pressured and where they could build each other up—Tuesday mornings at 8 am is an excellent sustainable time. I wasn't expecting many people to come as it was during the work week, but it suited what I could commit to every week. I'm a leader and an entrepreneur. I like to start things, think outside the box, and do things uniquely. I enjoy the challenge of being creative and finding solutions in a fun and unusual manner. However, I was nervous about starting this group. What if no one came? Would it reflect on me as a person? On me as a runner or physio if I couldn't even get a group of ladies together? I wrestled with these questions as I decided to start Wander Women. After much thought, I decided that it didn't matter. I would go running regardless if there were ten ladies or just myself. I would be satisfied but enjoy the journey, whether the group grew, stayed small, or didn't develop. It would not be a reflection of who I am. It seems simplistic, but how often do we wait to start something or focus on all the possible negatives rather than take the plunge no matter the outcome? I was investing a small amount of money. It was my time, and I would go for a run whether I had a group or not, so it would never be a waste.

In my heart of hearts, I wanted it to work, to grow – otherwise, I wouldn't have even started the group. But my outlook had changed to take the pressure off myself and enjoy the journey, whatever it looked like. I advertised on the usual social media platforms. I persuaded an incredible local artist to make a large board for me with the Wander Women logo so we could take a picture before each run. Our little mascot, Imbuzi the goat (made by the talented Traci Cowcandied), travels with us and shares in our adventures. The goat seemed like the perfect symbol for our group – resilient, cheeky, loving the trails, and quirky.

On Tuesday, the 5th of October 2021, at 8 am, we had our first Wander Women trail run at Morewood Farm in Hillcrest. Two ladies joined in – my friends Karen and Sbahle, who had driven up from Durban to join us. I was thrilled and, honestly, a bit relieved that the first run had more than just me. We set off onto the trails and ran/walked a 5 km mixture of the three trails on offer, stopping for pictures and a little dance routine captured on camera. It was amazing. Sbahle was new to trail running, and she fell in love with it – this was the beginning of a new adventure for her. After we finished, we celebrated at The Potter Shed with cake and coffee. I had sown the seeds for my little dream and it was starting to grow.

## UTCT 65 km 27 Nov 2021

The month leading up to my incredible race zoomed by. After my 50 km in 1000 Hills, the final taper ticked along with weekly runs and planning towards the big day. I was excited to go to Cape Town, stay with my family, and spend time with my sister who was visiting from America. I was so excited the night before the race that I had a restless but happy sleep. I woke up ready for the early morning start. My sister, Sue, kindly offered to get up at a stupid o'clock to drop me off at the beginning of the race at the Garden Tech Rugby Club. I chattered along, getting a little nervous but so thankful to have her support. It meant so much that she took the time to take me to the start, which calmed my nerves.

I re-checked all my gear, but there wasn't much I could do at this stage if I had forgotten something. Saying farewell to my sister, I made my way to the field, and that's when the vibe hit me. It was electrified despite the darkness and slight chill of the early morning air. Runners were buzzing around with nervous energy, music set the scene for a glorious morning, and there was such incredible energy. I entered the tent and met up with a few runners I knew or had met through social media. One of the biggest things I love about running is the community that it builds. The support, camaraderie, and the fact that it doesn't matter what your background or ability is —we're all in the same race, going through the same challenging parts. Another massive reason I love to run is that I have been given the incredible ability to run, and my body is strong and resilient. I want to use this privilege when so many others cannot. It brings me joy. Even during rough times, I recall that I chose to do this race, and I look up at the beauty surrounding me.

As I have run further into the ultra-distances, I've realised that you always feel different throughout the race. If you feel tired or deflated, the feeling will pass. Sometimes, we must problem-solve by eating more, hydrating, or napping. A kind word of encouragement goes a long way, and the power of the mind to make or break a run must not be underestimated. Throughout my training, I ensured I had the right physical tools for strength, conditioning, and time on the trails. Equally important was training my mind, emotions, and nutrition.

I did this with the race preparations. As soon as I entered the UTCT 65 km, I printed out the profile of the map, marked along the parts I knew, and asked for advice about the sections I didn't know much about and how best to tackle them. I looked up the previous times for the ladies to understand how long I might take. I aimed for the top 20 times as an estimate. I mimicked my training the best I could to the race and envisioned crossing the finish line, anticipating the highs and lows that I might have.

Nutrition formed a large part of my planning. I trained my nutrition strategies and played with different foods, gels, and liquid rehydrates. I quickly learned that I must eat early on—forward loading—and have a balance of more savoury than sweet foods. It is a good idea to have a variety of nutrition so that you don't get bored and nutrition that is easy to swallow. Later in my runs, I relied heavily on liquid nutrition—easy to get down.

The race day was finally here, and I felt prepared in every way possible. Standing at the start line, I took a deep breath and reminded myself of all the training, planning, and support that had brought me to this moment. I was ready to take on the UTCT 65 km and make the most of every step, every view, and every challenge along the way.

We bustled to the start line. I found my friend Chris, who had joined me in my crazy 1000 Hills Parkrun training, and we nervously stood in the chute. I knew I would only see him in the early parts of the race; he's a solid runner, consistently training with strength and speed. The music built, the announcer counted down, and three – two – one, we were off! We began our journey across the rugby field in the early morning, with headlamps lighting our way. It was an eerie quiet, filled with regular footsteps, as we shot out of the fields and soon turned down the dark roads. It was a fast downhill for a kilometre, and then we hit our first steep uphill. Chris slowly slipped away, and I reminded myself to run my race. I backed off my pace and was thankful to see other runners fast-walking up the steep tarred road. I joined them. In an ultra, you can never walk too early.

One piece of advice I was given from an ultra-running friend was to walk before you need to. Soon after the brief road section, we approached the twisty path that circumnavigates Signal Hill. We were at a steady pace, and I followed suit in a comfortable stride, with the other runners hemming me in front and behind on the single track through the scattered trees. The dawn of the first light meant we no longer needed our headlamps as we made our way up to the first aid station around 10 km. This was a quick pause to grab some fruit and continue. Soon afterwards, we climbed to the infamous Kloof Nek along the contour path to meet Platteklip. Steps and a steep climb to the summit of Table Mountain awaited us. It was misty, but we heard bagpipes playing in the mist as we climbed. It was mesmerising. I was hiking hard up the path but, at the same time, taking it all in. I kept anticipating seeing the musicians, but the music continued this morning. Eventually, we broke through the mist about halfway up the climb to find two bagpipe players. What a sight. A quick pic of a huge smile, and I continued my way to the top. This path is always longer than I anticipate. At this stage, we have completed over a half marathon (21 km), accumulating elevation with every step. At last, the narrow path reaching towards the glorious summit is seen.

The weather had turned bitterly cold, and my sudden elation for reaching the top turned to concern as my body felt crampy and completely fatigued. I recognised that I was both cold and had insufficient fuelling at this first energy-sapping stage. I quickly dressed in my waterproofs and stuffed my face with a total energy bar with a good dollop of rehydrate. Within ten minutes, I finally felt the energy returning, and I sighed in relief as I continued slowly making my way across the top of the slippery trails of Table Mountain. They are technical and can be hazardous when wet. I had decided early on—especially with the weather we were experiencing—to hike these sections rather than try running them and risk an early injury with a sprained ankle or worse. I had done these trails before and knew how wet and unpredictable they could be. I also knew that there were plenty of opportunities coming up to run efficiently rather than risk it now for a few extra minutes but a high risk of injury. Always weigh your choices based on the terrain, skill, and overall distance you must complete.

At this stage, the 35 km front runners started to pass us. I looked out for my friend Denzil, who had entered this race. They flew past, and it was a joy to see how they nimbly picked their way across the wet, slippery, and technical rocks and fynbos (a unique type of vegetation found only in the southern tip of Africa). Some of the 100 km runners were also making their way along, and I squealed with delight when I met Nontu Gabege, an incredible, powerful, and inspiring woman of strength and resilience.

We came to the scout hut at the far side of the mountain for our second aid station and were greeted by the most amazing scouts. The weather was still miserable, with drizzle and cold, but they welcomed us with smiles. I came through with my customary "whoop whoop," and who was at the station but Denzil! I couldn't believe it. What were the chances we would meet at this one point where the 35 km intersects the 65 km race? We exchanged hellos and then left the aid station together, but all too soon, we said farewell as the splits for the two different races took us on our different journeys.

The weather started to brighten up, and the rain lessened with the warmth of the sun's rays peeking through the sky. It promised to be a beautiful day despite the rather muggy start. We had reached the far side of Table Mountain and wound our way down a jeep track before dropping onto the Alphen trail. Suddenly, I felt a pang of emotion. I realised what I had already accomplished, having run over halfway into my race and feeling so good, knowing that my training had prepared my body and mind for this challenge. I felt overwhelmed as I remembered that a mere two years ago, I was released from the hospital after having my left hamstring completely reattached to my bone, not putting any weight on my left leg and having to use crutches. Knowing what a long journey it was to get to where I was, flying down the jeep track, I felt incredibly grateful for this body and what it had achieved despite the injury.

I had worked hard and trained hard. I consistently put in the hours of strength, mobility, and running to be in the most optimal condition and give it my best on race day. This was the reason for choosing this challenging race. We must show that we can accomplish much with perseverance, time, and hard work. We have to want it enough and work hard enough for it. Nothing worth having is easy because it wouldn't be worth it if it were.

I cried. The emotions had built up, and when I finally allowed myself to realise what I was accomplishing with everything I had gone through, I was so grateful to God and the knowledge I have as a physio and runner. To show that persistent strengthening and rehab work means you can return to a sport and thrive in it.

With my sunglasses on, I continued running solo through the vineyards. I often find myself between groups, not entirely with anyone, but always moving forward. We dropped into Newlands Forest from Alphen Trail, where the formidable steps awaited us along the contour path. Climbing more than I remembered, I encountered many 35 km runners and bumped into two friends along the route. A steep downhill led us to our last aid station at the University of Cape Town (UCT), where fuelling up was essential.

As I approached, the energy, music, and vibe were incredible. They welcomed us by name over the loudspeaker. The volunteers were terrific, filling bottles and offering a range of nutrition, from sandwiches to Bar One chocolates (similar to Mars bars, though, honestly, not quite the same!). I felt full of energy, renewed by every person I saw. Despite being tired, I was in much better form than expected at the 50 km.

The following section was familiar: a long, steep climb to the King's Blockhouse. Mentally preparing myself, I saw a familiar face, followed by a "WHOOHOO" – it was Brett, my brother. He had come to support and walk with me for part of the race, making me laugh endlessly. While I power-walked up, he kept pace, joking that he felt like he was dying, even though I was the one who had run so far. He shared encouraging messages from friends and family and took photos to update them on my progress. We said our farewells, and I climbed the last part up to the blockhouse, hands on knees, steady and robust.

The wind had picked up, blowing us around with surging gusts. I caught up to several 35 km runners snaking their way up the trail. The section was steep and single-track, so I asked to pass people as I steadily went faster up the hill. Then, I saw her – Courtney Dauwalter. I couldn't believe my eyes. She was the first lady, by a long way, in the 100 km race, climbing the hill as if it were downhill. With powerful strides, using her legs and arms, she gave her signature smile and a cheery American hello. Courtney is a huge inspiration to many women, especially in the ultra-running world, and she has accomplished so much. She whizzed past me, and I followed in her dust, thrilled to have met her briefly on the route.

The last section was along the contour path back down to the rugby grounds where we had started that morning. I ran comfortably until the wind surged, forcing me to walk until it faded. We hit Dead Man's Tree, knowing it wasn't much further. Winding down a rocky path, I emerged to the beautiful sight of more lovely supporters – Se7en and her family! A quick wave hello, a shriek of surprise, and with renewed energy, I burst forward to the final 5 km of the route.

The last section was a winding, uneven jeep track scattered with rocks of all sizes. I was careful, not wanting to risk injury after coming so far. The music grew louder, the scattered crowds grew into more giant clumps of supporters, and I finally went onto the field to run my victory loop – grinning from ear to ear as I completed my 65 km Ultra Trail Cape Town. A beer in hand and Denzil at the finish, having completed his 35 km – what a day. UTCT 65 km, 10 hr 40 min, 2932 m elevation, 11th lady, and first lady in my age group.

## The Post-Race Blues

After the UTCT 65 km race, I felt both pride and emptiness. The challenge had driven me, and doing so well gave me an emotional high. But once it was over, I felt aimless without a big goal to train for. This post-event letdown can be familiar, but it still hit hard. Life felt more arduous, and I struggled with questions about my small, slowly growing physio practice and purpose. I'm very goal-oriented, so being without specific goals made me feel off.

Balancing family life, training, and work was a constant struggle. I needed discipline to get up early, ensuring I had time for my family, but it left me often tired and irritable. The pull between training hard and meeting the needs of my family and friends was relentless. Time is the most important gift you can give someone, and I knew how much energy I was dedicating to my ultra-running goals.

During this rough patch, I reached out to friends and family for support and received these encouraging words:

*Hang in there. Find your happy place. You're a wonderful person with many friends.*

*Read a good novel for thirty minutes.*

*Think of you. Drop some less critical tasks. Have coffee with a friend.*

*You're unique and inspirational, humble. Thanks for sharing and being transparent. You've got this.*

*Pray for peace. Find time to unwind and breathe deeply.*

*Your dog understands you.*

*Talk to like-minded people. Ask for help; take it one day at a time. Hang in there.*

*Breathe, prioritise, and say thank you. Run barefoot. Spend time with family.*

*Everyone faces burnout. Breathe and take a step back.*

*Declutter and pause. Take time for yourself. Avoid toxic people. Pray and rest. You're stronger than you think.*

*Cut yourself some slack. Take it one hour at a time, one day at a time. Focus on what you've done right. Pray and be still.*

*Big hugs. Storm loves you. You give a lot of yourself. Prioritise, plan, and reflect.*

*Close your eyes. Ignore the noise. Take a deep breath and start again. Most things can wait or sort themselves out. Focus on yourself for a day.*

*Take an hour to chill.*

*You're amazing. Sometimes, things can't be perfect, and that's okay.*

*Don't apologise for being human. Thank you for being honest. Be kind to yourself.*

*Reaching out is the first step. Simplicity – how do we go back?*

*Give yourself grace.*

*Try taking it easy. Keep your chin up after every storm; it is an even more beautiful rainbow.*

*Step off the treadmill and redefine what's essential. Take a break, take a nap. You can take a break.*

*Thinking of you, and I love you.*

*Belt out some music in the car, and have a good cry before God. Know you're not alone; He's holding you up and working it out for good.*

*You cope just fine. The problem is the high standards you set for yourself. Sometimes good enough is okay, and saying "not right now" is essential for your mental health.*

*Sometimes, we need perspective and some loving friends' advice.*

These words of encouragement reminded me that I am not alone and it's okay to ask for help and take a break. Life's challenges are more accessible to face with the support of friends and family.

**The Next Big Goal**

UTCT announced a 100-mile race for 2022, and I knew I had to enter despite my fear. My confidence came from completing over 100 km during the 13 Peaks Challenge on similar terrain and elevation. This was possible with the proper training, mindset, crew, and support, even though it would take everything to finish.

The route description captivated me immediately: The 100-miler route spans from the northern mountain range of the Mother City to the remote southern mountains, including trails from Silvermine to Kalk Bay, Simon's Town,

Kommetjie, and Noordhoek. The race starts with a climb out of the city up to Signal Hill and around Lions Head, providing stunning views of the city and the Atlantic Seaboard. Runners climb midway up Table Mountain's north face and run a contour to Platteklip Gorge, the longest vertical ascent of the race, a notorious route with gradients exceeding 35 degrees, up Table Mountain. After 25 km, participants will have already covered an elevation gain of 1700 m.

Reaching the top of Table Mountain, runners traverse the famous tabletop ridge, then run along the magnificent 12 Apostles before taking on the technical descent of Llandudno Ravine, eventually arriving at Llandudno Aid Station. The route flattens out along the remote scenic coastal stretches of Sandy Bay and beyond. The second of the four steep climbs is the 600 m climb to Suther Peak and a traverse of Karbonkelberg to Hout Bay Aid Station.

Participants venture into the Southern Peninsula after leaving the Hout Bay Aid Station via East Fort and Blackburn Ravine, the third steep climb. Now running in the dark, participants can enjoy the runnable southern trails from Silvermine to Kommetjie Aid Station. Runners are rewarded with a flat 8 km beach section to stretch their legs from Kommetjie to Noordhoek. Participants then make their way along Chapman's Peak Drive to the start of their fourth significant climb up to Chapman's Peak. From here, it's homebound via Manganese Mines and Vlakenberg to Constantia Nek, where they head through the vineyards and city greenbelts to reach Alphen Trail Aid Station. There is still some climbing through technical sections of Cecilia and Newlands Forests, followed by a steep drop below Rhodes Memorial and the last Aid Station on the outskirts of the University of Cape Town.

The final 10 km requires digging deep with an intense climb to the Blockhouse and a lower traverse of Devil's Peak. Reaching it marks the home stretch and presents incredible views of the city, the Atlantic Ocean, Table Mountain, and Lions Head.

## UTCT

As soon as entries opened, I signed up for the inaugural 100-miler for Ultra Trail Cape Town at the end of November. No one had raced this yet so everything would be new. I knew it would be an extremely well-organised race, with well-marked trails, excellent aid stations, and support. I also had my winning formula: my seconders/support crew.

When they opened the entries in the morning, I ran with Denzil. We were chatting about the race. Well, Denzil was trying to decide which race to enter. After his UTCT 35 km and seemingly never doing another long one, the bug had certainly bitten! He chatted along the whole run – as I usually do most of the conversation – and eventually convinced himself to enter and run the 100 km! I laughed so loud. It went from discussing the pros and cons of the 55 km to how he would pass the 100 km, giving him FOMO (fear of missing out). Eventually, it finished with, "Okay, I'll enter the 100 km." I didn't even need to try and convince him! That afternoon, entries opened, and shortly after I hit the paid button, I received a message from Denzil with a picture of his 100 km entry. Looks like we both jumped our distances in a year! It's a good thing, as it is always more fun with training partners.

My excitement was building again as I started planning my year with big races and trail runs leading up to the 100-miler. I decided to enter the Comrades Ultra Marathon at the end of August as it would be a great stepping stone and training for my "A-goal" race, the 100-miler. It also meant that I could train with Rox as this would be her first Comrade, and I couldn't wait to be part of her journey to her first Comrades. It would make training much easier and more fun doing it together—team goals.

I decided to enter the Umgeni Marathon on the 13th of March to qualify for Comrades. I had heard a great deal about this marathon, and it comprised two out-and-back loops in opposite directions along the scenic water's edge of the Midmar Dam on undulating tar and gravel roads. My goal was to race as best I could and qualify for Comrades so I knew I could run it later in the year. I would then try a second marathon to see if I could get a better seeding later in the year with better training. It was a beautiful, warm morning. I was thankful for my cap and being used to running in the heat. I went out fairly conservatively, and the aim was to stay steady. I had not raced this distance for a long time, and my biggest concern was bombing out halfway – not having enough energy to continue correctly. As I turned around at the halfway point, soon afterwards, my incredible friend Marissa sped past! This was her first road marathon, and she was smashing it. I stayed consistent with my pacing, finishing in 3 hours and 48 minutes, earning me a podium in third place. What an incredible surprise. This also meant I had qualified for Comrades in the "D" batch. This marathon was challenging. I was not used to racing at pace for this amount of time, and my body took a beating. I felt fatigued afterwards but was thankful that within two or three days, my legs were starting to feel normal. Slight fatigue, but ready to continue training.

After my marathon, I decided to coach myself. I had learned a great deal from the two coaches I had been under, but I felt it was time to do my training, allowing me to be flexible and creative, especially with the massive goal of elevation and time on my feet that I was training towards. Planning for significant events excites me and is a large part of an athlete's success. I broke down each section of the race, considering different types of weather I might encounter and the gear I needed to test, and made a checklist to ensure I practised each aspect. I needed to test out my rain gear for an extended period and train for elevation. I had the perfect (initially unplanned) session for it!

**The Unplanned Perfect Session**

One weekend, I set out on a long training run, wondering what the weather would be like. As it turned out, it rained almost the entire time. This was ideal for testing my rain gear and seeing how it held up during prolonged exposure. The trail was muddy and slick, simulating the conditions I might face during the UTCT 100-miler. I had packed all my essential gear, including extra layers, snacks, and trusty poles, crucial for navigating steep and slippery sections.

The run was tough. The rain was relentless, and the terrain was challenging, but it was precisely what I needed. I made mental notes on what worked well and what needed adjustment. My rain jacket held up nicely, but my shoes struggled with the mud, so I needed a different pair for race day. The session was a great confidence booster, reinforcing my ability to adapt and persevere through demanding conditions.

## Training Highlights and Adjustments

Throughout my self-coaching journey, I focused on several key areas:

- **Elevation Training**: I incorporated hill repeats and long runs with significant elevation gain, mimicking the race's demanding profile. Living in an area with rolling hills made this part more straightforward.

- **Gear Testing**: I meticulously tested all my gear in various conditions. This included running in different weather scenarios, testing hydration packs, nutrition strategies, and ensuring my clothing was comfortable for long distances.

- **Nutrition and Hydration**: I experimented with various nutrition plans, ensuring I had a mix of savoury and sweet options to avoid palate fatigue. Hydration strategies were crucial, especially for the long, hot sections of the race.

- **Mental Preparation**: I visualised different parts of the race, prepared for potential low points, and developed strategies to stay positive and focused. This included running loops to build mental resilience and practising mindfulness techniques.

## Building Towards the Goal

As the race day approached, I felt increasingly prepared. My comprehensive training covered all the essential aspects needed to tackle the 100-miler. Combining self-coaching, rigorous planning, and thorough gear testing gave me confidence. I knew the journey ahead would be challenging, but I was ready to face it head-on with a solid plan and the determination to see it through. The unplanned rainy training session was pivotal, reinforcing the importance of adaptability and thorough Preparation. Each run, each piece of gear tested, and every mental strategy developed brought me one step closer to my ultimate goal.

## Half Everesting for Fit4Rhino: 21 May 2022

As part of my training for my first 100-miler, I was on the lookout for events that would help me train effectively, especially those that offered substantial elevation gains. In Durban, we have plenty of technical trails with steep climbs, but most are short or involve looping, which can get monotonous. My priority was finding an event with significant elevation, and that's when a great friend, Liezl Schoeman, introduced me to one of her passions: raising funds for baby rhinos through her Fit4Rhino campaign.

Liezl's event aimed to promote #fitnesswithpurpose, raising much-needed funds for emergencies relating to feeding baby rhinos, veterinarian costs, daily management, security, and private rhino conservation initiatives for selected charity partners. The campaign hashtag, #REMEMBERTHEMILK, focused on supporting Rhino Babies (orphans) through the Rhino Connect NPO, which looks after 3,000 rhinos from private farms and reserves in South Africa, including several orphaned calves. We aimed to raise funds to procure milk and milk products for these little ones.

Liezl organised a weekend of Everesting events—activities where participants ascend and descend a given hill multiple times until they've climbed the equivalent height of Mount Everest (8,848 metres). There were options for runners, cyclists, and swimmers. Knowing my love for ultra-running and new challenges, she invited me to participate in the South African national Everesting event to raise funds for Fit4Rhino. I aimed for a half Everesting, which meant ascending 4,428 metres—a great training opportunity for my 100-miler, which would also involve significant elevation.

The date was set for Saturday, 21st May. As the weekend approached, I began obsessively checking the weather, crucial for planning and preparing for the day. It looked like it would be cold and rainy—perfect conditions for testing my gear, but I was concerned it might deter supporters from coming out. I needn't have worried; the support was more than I expected.

The key to a successful Everesting event is choosing a safe, accessible trail with decent elevation that you can repeat. I selected Honey Trails, a nearby location with ample parking and good support. The only challenge was the 1.5 km walk down to the starting point at the top of the peak, where we had to carry all our gear. From there, we descended to the bottom of the trail—a series of massive switchbacks—before starting our first ascent. I had scouted the route a few weeks before measuring it and calculating the required ascents. It was going to be a long, demanding day!

I started solo in the early hours, battling horrible weather from start to finish. I arrived at Honey Trails by myself at 5 a.m. It was pouring rain, pitch dark, and cold. I second-guessed my decision to attempt this challenge on such a day. But I had already committed — I shared my plans on social media, invited friends to join, and asked people to donate to the cause. Backing out wasn't an option. Besides, I couldn't just turn around if race day presented the same conditions. I knew this was a vital opportunity to toughen up mentally and physically and test my gear and nutrition under challenging conditions.

The first hour was quiet, spent alone in the dark and rain. Despite the miserable weather, I found a strange enjoyment in the solitude. Soon, a few friends joined in, braving the torrential rain and wind alongside me. Their company re-energized me, and as more friends arrived, I felt a renewed sense of purpose despite the relentless weather.

Then, I faced a dilemma—I desperately needed to wee. I tried holding it, but it was becoming unbearable. Returning to the house wasn't an option; it would waste too much time. But by now, quite a few people were on the mountain, going up and down. I had to go. I decided to head to the bottom, found a spot slightly shielded by trees, and hoped for a quick, discreet pit stop.

What I imagined as a simple task turned into a struggle with wet clothing. Instead of a quick squat and go, it became a battle—pulling, wriggling, and fighting to get my tights down without tearing them, squatting while trying not to get blown over, and then the arduous task of pulling the soaked tights back up, which clung to my legs like glue. Thankfully, I managed to do all this without anyone stumbling upon the scene, and the relief was immense—both mentally and physically

Rox stayed with me until the end, climbing alongside me and ensuring we packed up and got home safely, which made me feel loved and supported. The turnout of friends who came to cheer me on, run a few loops, or feed me in the pouring rain was overwhelming. It just shows how committed and excellent the running community is. I thought the weather would deter many, but the support was felt deeply despite the rain.

I'm grateful for the gear that kept me warm and dry for most of the day, but after 12 hours in pouring rain, wind, and mud, I reached the point where enough was enough.

Unfortunately, I had to call it quits at 6 p.m., 12 hours after I started, because the hill at Honey Trails was becoming dangerously slippery, even with poles. I didn't want to risk the safety of my friends, who stayed with me, as the temperature plummeted. If I had twisted my ankle at the bottom of the hill, getting back up could have been a severe ordeal. I was immensely thankful for the incredible support throughout the day. Despite the relentless rain, wind, and cold, several friends joined me for a lap or three, making it all much more accessible to bear. But those last few hours were tiring, and in the end, safety had to come first. Initially, I hiked hard on the ups and jogged the downs, but by the end, even going down was difficult. A mini river had formed on the trail, making it more slippery and unpredictable. With the cold, rain, and darkness setting in, it was time to make the sensible decision to call it a day.

This challenge was a great mental and physical test for me, setting me up as one of my key training sessions leading to the success of my 100 milers. This experience taught me the importance of changing into seamless underwear to avoid chafing (definitely not fun!) and investing in better gloves for the cold. After consulting with some experienced trail runners, I bought three pairs of gloves for various conditions. I also confirmed that my waterproof jacket was comfortable and my poles were invaluable. Testing your gear, especially in ultra running, is vital. It can make or break your experience—imagine dealing with chafing for 10 to 20 hours or longer; there's only so much cream you can apply.

I completed 55.66 km in 12 hours and 32 minutes, with 3,708 metres of elevation.

Driving home was nerve-wracking. Rox took a different route, and the streets were waterlogged with massive puddles. It took me a long time to get home safely, and at one point, the rain was so heavy I could barely see out the windscreen. I was incredibly thankful to get home safely, shower, and collapse into bed.

I was also really impressed with my friend Denzil, who, while travelling through George, summited George Peak four times, inspired by local legend Jacques Mouton and his mental toughness. Denzil completed his half-everesting and also raised much-needed money for the rhinos. This challenge reaffirmed that while the physical aspect of ultra-running is crucial, the mental aspect needs even more training. This mental toughness is developed through physical exercise and careful planning leading up to and on race day.

## Change

In the middle of June, everything began to shift in ways I couldn't have predicted. Glen and I had casual conversations about moving to the United

Kingdom in the next few years, so I researched online to see what job opportunities were available.

There were plenty of reasons driving us to consider this move. Living in KwaZulu-Natal (KZN), South Africa, we endured an adamant couple of years. First, we endured extreme looting that came frighteningly close to our home. We could hear gunfire in the distance, and there were constant updates about the looters' movements and the chaos unfolding. It was a time when many big and small businesses were destroyed. Shops were ransacked, and people took advantage of the situation to grab whatever they could.

Meanwhile, our neighbourhood watch was our lifeline, keeping a close eye on our community. We were essentially trapped in our homes, surrounded by the constant threat of violence. Essentials like milk and bread quickly disappeared from the shelves, and the roads were blocked with burning tyres. It was a terrifying few days.

The following year brought more devastation with floods that KZN had never experienced on such a scale. Lives were lost, and the damage was catastrophic, with millions of rands worth of property destroyed. Even months later, many homes were still waiting for insurance companies to assess the damage and begin rebuilding. We were incredibly fortunate—our house was spared, with only minor flooding in the garden and a small sinkhole near our neighbour's wall that was easily fixed, thanks to Glen's diligence in maintaining the gutters.

Others were not so lucky. Our friends had their homes filled with mud and debris, with cars stuck wheel-deep in the muck. Their house was inundated, and their backyard was a disaster zone, with collapsed walls and mud everywhere. I spent a morning helping to dig out their home, trying to salvage what we could. The community came together during this time. People who had never spoken before now worked side by side, offering help, food, and a place to stay. It was heartwarming to see how people rallied together in the face of such devastation, breaking down social barriers and supporting each other.

During this period, I ran around our area, which had become almost unrecognisable. The roads were so covered in mud and water that I had to wear my trail shoes to navigate them. Half-destroyed buildings lined the streets, and people were out trying to recover what they could from the wreckage. I spoke to one business owner whose shop had been half-washed away by the floodwaters. He was salvaging whatever he could, but the loss was immense.

Lives were lost as walls collapsed, swimming pools were uprooted and dumped into neighbouring properties, and foundations crumbled under the pressure of the water. Roads were destroyed, creating traffic nightmares and fraying nerves as the slow rebuilding process began. Repairs had not started in many areas, so the community stepped in to make things safer. Despite being safe and spared the worst damage, I felt restless. The destruction around us, the sense of vulnerability, and the uncertainty of the future weighed heavily on me. It became clear that moving overseas might not just be an idea for the distant future but something we needed to consider more seriously—for a change, an adventure, and, most importantly, the opportunities it could offer our children.

"Head of Rehab" at Pure Sports Medicine caught my eye as I browsed Job Escalator—a platform for physiotherapy jobs in the UK. The salary was appealing, and the role itself—hold on, it was perfect! Part clinical, meaning I'd still be treating patients as a physio, and part management, offering the flexibility to oversee others, learn, and manage the rehabilitation side alongside a team. The more I read about the requirements, the more it felt like this job was tailor-made for my personality, experience, and expertise. It was in the sports field, surrounded by a multidisciplinary team of sports clinicians based in London—one area we considered. The role included teaching, conducting annual appraisals, and opportunities to explore projects that would allow me to make the role my own.

## I applied.

My philosophy is to seize opportunities. Even though this was a large company, likely with internal candidates, and I was based in South Africa while most applicants would be in the UK, I'd never have a chance if I didn't apply. But if I did use it, who knew what could happen? I sent off my CV, but only after enlisting the help of my brother and sister to craft the accompanying letter. How could I convey my enthusiasm, zest for life, and passion for sports? I knew many others would have similar work experience and qualifications, so I needed to stand out. I highlighted each part of the job application that Pure Sports Medicine had outlined—I run my physio practice, have taught and supervised physio students in hospital settings, and hold a master's degree and a diploma in orthopaedic medicine.

The key, in my mind, was sharing my passion for founding Wander Women— a women's only weekly trail running group that had been thriving for a year— and my running assessment service, which I'd successfully used with my runners.

## Within two weeks, my life changed.

After an online interview, I was offered the job! Despite applying, I genuinely didn't expect to get it. I was thrilled, shocked, and plunged into a whirlwind of planning. The next question was, when could I start? After discussing it with Glen and considering that the Comrades Ultra Marathon was only three weeks away, I asked if it would be possible to begin in the new year. Otherwise, I'd have to uproot my entire life by the beginning of October.

October was set. In just five weeks, I went from running my practice and living in Durban to buying flight tickets, wrapping up my practice, informing friends and family, and tackling an enormous amount of admin to move to London.

We decided that Glen and the kids would join me in the new year once the school year had finished, things had settled, and I'd found a home for us. I had also committed to launching the inaugural Upper Highway Trail Marathon (UHTM) as one of its five organisers in December and to my mammoth challenge—the UTCT 100 miler at the end of November. So, although I was starting in October, my new employers agreed that I could return to South Africa for these events, wrap up my life in Durban, and then return to London in the new year.

But first, I had the not-so-small task of running 90 km from Pietermaritzburg to Durban for my third Comrades Ultra Marathon—and keeping the news of my immigration under wraps from my best friend until after the big day. That was one of the most complex decisions I've ever made.

**Comrades Ultra Marathon – 28 August 2022**

Roxie has become my best friend. Since she took on the unique trail puzzle, I created during lockdown and joined me for the X-Berg challenge, we just clicked—we thrive on our shared craziness. At the beginning of the year, I decided to take on the 100-miler, but it's always good to have interim goals. We often refer to coaching and planning races as A and B races. Rox was preparing for her first Comrades this year, so I joined her in training. My training was a bit unconventional, incorporating a lot of trail and elevation alongside the long road runs in my weekly programme.

This year's Comrades would be spectacular, especially since it was the 95th race, with a special medal to mark the occasion. The event had been put on hold for two years due to the COVID pandemic, so this was not only the 95th Comrades but also a significant comeback. This would be my third Comrades, completing my first in 2017 and back-to-back in 2018.

Comrades is usually held in June, but the organisers moved it to the end of August due to COVID restrictions. There were concerns that the weather might be too hot, being in KZN, but the date was set, and we planned accordingly.

Living in the area, we're fortunate to have access to many experienced runners who have completed numerous Comrades Ultras. Like any race, you gradually increase your mileage, and there's a "route tester" that's highly recommended, especially if it's your first time. Dean of Beloved Long Run fame organises the route tester, and it's a 56 km run from Pietermaritzburg to Hillcrest, with water tables—an unofficial race. Of course, you can do this independently, but it's much better with others, and Dean's event is so well organised.

We're lucky to live along the Comrades route, so we regularly run sections of it, which helps enormously mentally. The more I do ultra running, the more I realise that mental preparation can sometimes be even more critical than physical prep—or at least equally important. Many athletes neglect this crucial aspect. There will be challenging moments—how do you prepare mentally to keep going? Why are you running this race, and what motivates you to push through?

Leading up to Comrades, there's the registration, and I wanted to make it as unique for Rox as possible. Getting to the start line of the world's oldest ultramarathon is a considerable achievement!

As a fun reminder and celebration, we decided to get matching nails done in Comrades colours, along with our kit. We had a blast choosing designs and spending the afternoon together getting them professionally done.

Next was the registration at the ICC (International Conference Centre) in Durban. We were excited from the start. Rox and I have interesting car navigation skills. I was driving with Rox, trying to figure out where the entrance to a car park was. It wasn't easy to negotiate! Eventually, after circling the ICC a few times, we found the entrance and parked.

When we arrived, we spotted Dean's unmistakable cream soda-decorated car, so we went over to say hello. Always greeted with his cheery smile and trademark "hello hello," we then entered the hall for registration. It was quiet since we chose to go on Thursday afternoon, the first registration day. We collected our packs and proudly donned our Comrades peak caps.

Experience is often what you make of it. We can be in a seemingly dull place or activity, but I'm learning that it's often the people you're with, the attitudes, and the "funness" that create incredible memories. And that's precisely what we did!

The day was filled with laughs, from visiting the stand with the massage guns and pretending we were James Bond on a secret mission to filming each other dancing up and down the escalators. But the most memorable part of my morning, at least for me, was in the Comrades Novice section. This area is designated for first-time Comrades runners. Rox and I (yes, I snuck in— sometimes it's all about who you know!) wandered in and noticed a TV displaying the Comrades route. I suggested Rox walk us through the route, but neither realised it was an interactive TV show! As Rox began showing us the route, she accidentally touched the screen, and suddenly, with a whooshing sound, the display changed. I've never seen someone jump so quickly, wondering what on earth was happening! It was hilarious, and the best part is I captured it all on camera—check it out on Instagram!

The early morning alarm went off at 1 am, and Glen took me to Durban to catch a bus to Pietermaritzburg, where the race would start. The bus was filled with quiet nerves; everyone was lost in their thoughts. We arrived with plenty of time to spare—the pens where we lined up according to our seeding weren't even open yet!

Once the pens opened, we lined up according to our batches. I was in C batch, while Rox was in D. I decided to stay in my batch rather than run together so we could each run our race. I knew I'd see Rox at some point—she had trained hard and was a strong runner. The crowds grew, the music played, and nerves heightened. The weather was perfect—cool but not cold. As the start time drew nearer, we bunched closer together, anticipating the final songs that signal the start of the race: *Chariots of Fire*, the cock crow, and *Shosholoza*. Then the gun fired—and we were off!

**This was the most emotional race I've ever run.**

I had already accepted my job in the UK, but I hadn't told anyone about it apart from Glen because I wanted to focus on the Comrades race and allow Rox, especially, to enjoy her well-earned race. I had trained hard, but I was disappointed that my legs felt like lead early on. I had paced myself well, hoping they'd warm up, but they didn't. Then my stomach felt unsettled—I tried to go to the toilet but couldn't. A stitch started and lasted for 15 km, no matter what I tried to do to get rid of it. I just kept on persevering, trying to make the best of it. I walked many more hills than planned, shifting my focus from a possible Bill Rowan (sub-9 hours) to simply finishing. The support along the route was out of this world, with friends and strangers offering everything—from salt to potatoes to jelly sweets.

Cramps began in my calves and thighs—not severe enough to stop me, but a gentle reminder that if I pushed too hard, they'd come back with a vengeance. Eventually, they calmed down but left my legs feeling weak and drained.

In Hillcrest, where the route finally starts to descend, I met up with several friends but was not at my best. I fixed a smile, feeling hugely grateful to see them. As I went through Kloof and then Gillitts, I heard a familiar singing voice behind me—it was Rox, super chirpy. We said hello and snapped a quick pic, and I encouraged her to carry on as I wasn't in a great space, and she was much stronger than me. After some reluctance, she slowly disappeared into the distance, and I felt relieved to continue at my own pace.

I pushed on, and I'll never forget Lindsay's words in Westville. Lindsay, who has her green number for Comrades—having run it ten times—speaks with the voice of experience. She grabbed me, shoved a hot cup of tea into my hand, and told me to drink up, then carry on down the hill. There's nothing like a hot cup of tea in the middle of an ultra! The key is to keep moving—whether walking or running—rather than to stop.

Another significant moment was with Tracey. We had been passing each other back and forth, and I had decided to walk again on a downhill. She passed me, but not before leaving a very pertinent message after I complained that my legs were aching (not a massive surprise over 70 km into the race!).

**These Five Words Changed My Race:**

**"Now. You have to FIGHT."**

And fight I did! At that moment, I decided I could run down the hills. It was just pain, after all. I walked the ups, staggered along the flats, and found my groove. The highlight of my day came in the home stretch when I saw Moses Mabhida Stadium in the distance. It felt like it would never come closer, but then I saw a familiar runner ahead of me—Rox! I couldn't believe it! I shouted her name repeatedly, but she didn't hear me. We had only 2 kilometres to go. I dug deep, found a little burst of speed—what felt like my best sprint ever— and caught up to her! We rejoiced, and I knew she wouldn't want to slow down, so we steadily increased our pace in those final kilometres. We finished hand in hand, crossing the finish line together. Friends who had trained together finished together. It was an extremely emotional and proud moment for me. Rox, on her first Comrades, had done exceedingly well. The stadium crowds were loud, drawing us on. We took our time in the chute, taking photos of our medals, savouring the moment of being together after completing 90 kilometres in 9 hours 32 minutes, with 1174 metres of elevation.

But then we had to face the enormous stairs to exit the stadium. Runners adopted various strategies to get up—some side-stepping, others hauling themselves up using the railing. We made our way up slowly and finally emerged at the top. I felt utterly exhausted while my chirpy friend was still on cloud 55! After the race, I felt restless. I needed to find a toilet, which wasn't too far away. That's when I discovered blood in my urine, which was concerning. I'd read that the effort of running could cause this, but I made a mental note to keep an eye on it in case it worsened and required medical attention.

We joined Roxie's fellow club members in the stands. She looked like she had hardly run while I was hobbling around, feeling grumpy. As I sat down, all I could think about was getting home. I cried. I had held my secret for so long, and all the emotions came tumbling out. I felt sad watching friends complete this gruelling ultra marathon, knowing this would be my last Comrades. My feelings were torn between the excitement of a new adventure, work, and travel in the UK and the heartache of leaving behind so many friends, family, and the incredible communities I was a part of. Rox probably thought I was crying out of sheer relief from completing the Comrades, but it was so much more than that. I still held on to the secret, knowing I needed to tell her as soon as we got back to my home.

Finally, when we got home, I told Rox the news that I was leaving for the UK. It was a bittersweet end to the day, but I needed to let her know so I could move on, plan, and prepare. She was still full of endorphins from the race, so it didn't quite sink in initially. Poor Rox went through every emotion—from disbelief to being upset to frustration that I hadn't told her earlier. I explained why I had waited until after Comrades so she could focus on her first race without any additional worries. From being on an absolute high, I felt sad to have dropped this news on her. Later that evening, as things settled, the reality of my leaving began to sink in…this would be so hard for both of us!

**What I realised from my run, and any considerable event or challenge, is this:**
- You have to want it.
- It may go differently than planned.
- Deal with it.

- Just keep moving forward.
- Change the plan if needs be...
- And FIGHT for it!

**Family and Faith**

I haven't mentioned much about my family or God, but that doesn't mean these two aspects aren't central to my life. I'm a Christian, and I believe in Jesus. Without Him, I wouldn't be where I am today. He's the source of my strength, drive, and stubbornness to strive for the best. He fills me with joy, peace, and more blessings than I can count. He restores my soul and gives me hope when I have none left.

Before 2019, I went through the darkest time of my life due to personal difficulties. I wasn't sure how I'd come out on the other side or what that would look like. During those times, I took life an hour at a time, praying and hoping for positive outcomes and changes in myself. One of my biggest lessons was to hold on and fight for what you believe in. It's crucial to give your all, consider every angle, seek advice from wise friends and professionals, and, above all, cling to hope. Gradually, healing began. Trust was restored, and hope blossomed into daily changes, bringing blessings beyond what I could have imagined. I grew more robust, and we grew more assertive.

I'm the first to admit I'm far from perfect. I'm loud, opinionated, and full of many other attributes, but I love deeply and will always fight for what I believe in. I'm also willing to learn, to say sorry, and to change my opinion when I've been wrong. Everyone has their flaws. Social media only shows a curated version of someone's life, but I want transparency. I make stupid, careless mistakes, but I try my best to apologise, move on, and make things right where I can. Sometimes, I need to step away from negative situations to protect myself.

As I get older, I realise how important it is to live fully and use every minute to the best of my ability. I enjoy the mundane, share it, and aim to inspire others to dream big and pursue their goals. I trust in God, even when I don't understand the reasons behind certain situations. Looking back, I see how His hand guided me through my struggles.

## My Family

Being away from my family for ten weeks has been incredibly tough. It's been a long time since I was apart from my husband, two small children, close friends who are like family, and my beloved training partner, Storm, our gorgeous border collie. Keeping busy has helped me not to dwell too much on the distance, but I've missed physical contact—hugs—so acutely while here in England. I haven't yet made many friends, and when I video call Glen and the kids and see them hugging and jumping on him, it brings a lump to my throat. It's hard. For Glen, it's been equally challenging. He's had the immense task of selling our home, looking after the kids, and dealing with the day-to-day grind. While I'm adapting to an entirely new environment, Glen navigates the familiar but with the added strain of doing it all alone. We both cope with change differently. I seem to adapt more quickly, enjoying the challenge of setting up in new places, while Glen finds the whole process extremely stressful, with endless "to-do" lists on top of cooking, cleaning, and sorting the kids.

I've mistakenly compared our experiences, but recently, I've focused on being thankful and expressing that to Glen. I've thanked him for all he's done, which has drawn us closer. I recently listened to a podcast that has changed my thinking, especially in how I listen and respond in relationships and work. It emphasised the importance of genuinely listening without interruption and ensuring you understand the other person before responding. I've learned to be slower to formulate answers and quicker to listen and acknowledge. This podcast also suggested that when two distinct ideas seem to clash, there's often a third, mutually beneficial solution that might be even better. This has helped me see Glen's point of view more clearly and stop focusing so much on my needs. As a result, he's become more aware of what I'm going through and expressed how proud he is of how I've managed to set so much up here in England.

You're right. We often hold back from saying the things that truly matter, thinking them but never verbalising them. It's essential to be honest and open with each other, affirming and uplifting those around us. Whether it's telling a friend how beautiful they look, sharing a special moment with your child, or simply apologising for being tired after a long day—it all matters. Being natural, honest, and raw is not something to fear. What have you got to lose?

When I interviewed for my job in England, I clarified that what you see is what you get. I had nothing to lose and wanted them to know exactly who I was. That way, if they chose me, they knew what they were getting. It's worked out so well—I've slotted into the company smoothly, and our values align, which I was upfront about from the start. Friends and family often tell me they always know where they stand with me because I'm straightforward. I say it as it is. Of course, sometimes I don't get it right. I might not phrase something well, or my tone might be off, but that's all part of learning and growing. The key is to keep striving to communicate better next time.

# Phase 4: Taper

**London Bound**

**Farewell South Africa**

Packing up your life in just five weeks and saying goodbye to everyone you love is no easy feat. My only comfort was knowing I'd be back in nine weeks for my 100-miler. It was a whirlwind of decluttering, giving notice at work, selling off what I could, and packing everything else. I put all my belongings into one room at home to make it easier for Glen to sort through, and then I had to pack not just for London but also for my 100-miler! It was a mammoth task.

There were so many things to sort out—making sure my bank cards would work in the UK, selling off items, and clearing out the house to make it easier for Glen, especially since he had to put the house on the market. The hardest part was telling my friends and family. Some of my Wander Women were in tears when I broke the news; emotionally, it was incredibly difficult for me. But I kept going, staying busy with all the planning and packing, which didn't leave me much time to dwell on the goodbyes.

One of the most memorable moments was with my "Supamoms" group—a close-knit circle of friends who came together when our children were babies. We've supported each other through thick and thin, and for the past four years, we've had an annual weekend getaway together, just us, no kids. They spoiled me on our last night with laughter, love, and the most touching gifts and words. These friends are more than just friends—they're family. They've offered wisdom, advice, and chocolate for me at my lowest points.

I also had to let my physio patients know I was leaving and recommend two other physios to take over. Many of them already knew from social media, and their responses were overwhelmingly positive and supportive, which was encouraging. When we told our children about the move, sharing the news with them first was essential. Their reactions were interesting—Joshua was very matter-of-fact, already thinking about sorting out his Lego to sell, while Jen had a few tears and said she would miss family and friends. But they both took it well overall. We explained how different things would be and how we would go on this adventure together, making new friends and exploring new countries as a family. Kids can be resilient, often adapting more quickly than we give them credit. They focus on the present, and there's a lot we can learn from that.

As the move became more certain with dates, I contacted the school to give notice, and we arranged for Josh and Jen to attend aftercare, making things easier for Glen during the week. Then came planning for Storm, our border collie. I contacted an agency to handle his move, which involved getting blood tests for rabies, sorting out the necessary paperwork, and getting him used to the travel crate. All these little details took a lot of time, energy, and money, but they were essential in making the transition as smooth as possible.

In the weeks leading up to my move to the UK, one of the most important things for me was to spend quality time with friends and family. Those quiet coffee chats and early morning runs became essential amid all the busyness, packing, and sorting. They helped me stay balanced, calm, and maintain perspective. I was often asked how I felt about everything, which was a tricky question. It all felt quite sudden, yet it was clear this was the right path for us. We had prayed about it, and every door seemed to open wide with opportunity.

The job offer was well-suited to me, with a salary allowing us to settle in without too many worries. I felt excited rather than nervous, and the sheer amount of tasks to be done kept my mind occupied, leaving little time to dwell on the emotional weight of the move and its permanence. We've moved before, and I'm someone who embraces change and makes the most of every situation. While there are always people, places, and routines that we will miss, I love the thrill of discovering new places and embarking on new adventures. It's about looking forward while cherishing the past.

All too soon, the day arrived for me to leave for Cape Town—first to see my parents and brother and then to head off to London. Little did I know that the time I had left before this giant leap was even shorter than I had initially planned.

## Cape Town

I flew into Cape Town, greeted by the stunning mountain ranges below as a beautiful day unfolded. My plan was simple: a relaxed day with my parents and brother, enjoying a local coffee shop and brunch together. With such a short visit, I hadn't planned to see many other friends. Instead, I focused on spending quality time with Brett at our favourite local coffee spot, Come Brew Kenilworth. The two guys who run the place treat you like family, offering impeccable service and the most aromatic coffee options paired with mouthwatering snacks and light meals.

Brett and I caught up on family matters and life in general. We've always had a special bond despite me being the annoying little sister. When we were still living at home, he often helped me with my maths homework, and I'd share my chocolate stash with him as a thank you. I've always admired him, especially for his incredible talent in the English language and acting through Theatresports. Our relationship is built on raw honesty, and he doesn't hesitate to put me in my place or share differing perspectives, which I often need to hear. Both Brett and my sister understand me on a level that requires no explanation—we grew up in the same home, just a few years apart.

During our time together, Brett was going through a lot, and listening felt good. I didn't offer advice, but simply being there for him, letting him know he was heard without judgement, felt important. For me, time is one of the greatest gifts we can give—it's something we can never get back. I deeply value when people make time for me, and I've noticed it's often the busiest people who manage to do so.

Later, we took our parents out for lunch and had a wonderful time together. It reminded me that no matter a person's age, if you want to spend time with them, you shouldn't hesitate to make the coffee or lunch date happen. Age isn't always a predictor of how long someone will be around, so it's important to cherish those moments while you can.

My brother taught me a valuable lesson early on in my teenage years. I complained about not having enough time to do something, and he said,

**"You need to make the time because we all have the time."**

Let that sink in. Since then, I've adopted this mindset, and now I say that I haven't *made* time for something rather than claiming I don't have the time. We all have the same 24 hours in a day. How we choose to fill it, who we spend it with, and what we accomplish is entirely up to us. It's about our daily choices.

While sometimes we're stuck in situations for a period, we still have choices. It often comes down to how badly we want to change and how willing we are to work towards it. Slowly but surely, we start to see the changes we desire. This is true in life and in running. The first step is believing in your ability to change and work towards something you desperately want to achieve. Along the way, you gather incredible people who support you, especially when you doubt yourself. They quietly remind you of the truth, and because you trust them, you begin to believe in yourself again.

It's okay to doubt, to question. Just don't dwell on it. Remember why you chose to make the change or take on the challenge in the first place. Keep that reason close, and let it guide you back on track.

By the afternoon, I attempted to check in for my flights but was met with an alarming message: **my flights had been cancelled.** At first, it felt unreal—how could they cancel a flight just 24 hours before departure? But it happened. I tried phoning the airline but couldn't reach anyone. Then, I attempted to rebook a flight online, but there were only options for that evening or two days later, meaning landing in London on Friday and starting work on Monday. Not the best first impression.

I tried to rebook, but the system kept giving me error codes. At one point, I thought I had successfully booked new flights, but no confirmation email came through. When I checked again, it seemed I had indeed booked a flight for that evening—just a few short hours away. I had no confirmation or number to contact, and it appeared that the flight was indeed booked, so I needed to rush to the airport. During this time, my brain was in overdrive. I tried to stay cool, calm, and rational, thinking of the worst-case scenario—I'd start work late. Not ideal, but survivable. I rapidly packed all my belongings, said a quick and bewildered farewell to my parents, who were just as shocked as I was, and made my way to the airport. At the airport, I eventually found a number for the airline on one of the windows. After speaking with a lady, she confirmed that I had been booked on that evening's flight, scheduled for midnight. I was so relieved that I had made it to the airport! What a last-minute scramble. After checking in, I found a restaurant to grab dinner and gather my thoughts. My heart finally calmed down, knowing I had a valid passport and a boarding pass in hand—I must have checked it 50 times. Alone in a café, I felt a mixture of loneliness and excitement. I had missed out on a planned day in Cape Town, but at least I had seen my family and a few friends in the short time I had been there. Despite the frustration, I was thankful to have a flight and that it wouldn't delay my start date.

I also had to adjust my accommodation plans quickly, but fortunately, they could take me a day earlier. My mind raced with "to-do" lists, but all I could do now was sit on the flight and make my way to London. I thought I had everything sorted for my new job starting in five days... but there was one final hurdle I had yet to anticipate before I could begin work.

## First weeks in London

My first weeks in London were a whirlwind. The flights went smoothly, and I arrived at Woolwich Arsenal in southeast London, where I was lucky enough to find a room with John and David, thanks to a friend sharing my plea for accommodation. Housing in London is a nightmare—barely any is available, and what there is costs a fortune. But from the moment I arrived, I felt so welcomed by John and David. They usually rent out their room for a few days at a time, not nine weeks, but they were incredibly accommodating.

The area was lovely, with new upgrades and convenient shops just around the corner. The fresh Elizabeth Line (or Lizzy Line) and the Docklands Light Rail (DLR) were only eight minutes from the front door, making it easy to get to central London, notably Bank, where I'd be working. I felt so grateful to have found a home base with easy access to everything.

I ran along the Thames Path on my first evening to clear my head. The cool air and bright lights were just what I needed. I focused on the rhythm of my feet hitting the pavement, letting everything else wait until tomorrow. I still had some crucial tasks, like confirming a registration and getting a new bank card. I thought these would be straightforward, but I was wrong—they nearly caused a delay in my work start date!

I'm a list maker. I write down everything that needs to be done and tick off items as I complete them. So, it's incredibly frustrating when I spend ages ticking off an item only for it to reappear on my list. That's precisely what happened with my Chartered Society of Physiotherapy (CSP) registration, which I needed before starting work on Monday—it was already Friday!

This registration-required payment through a British bank account, which I didn't have because my card had expired. After many back-and-forth emails, they allowed me to pay via PayPal. Great, except PayPal wouldn't accept either of my South African bank accounts. I tried to think of a solution, and luckily, my sister stepped in and paid the fee for me. I sent the proof of payment and thought I was all set.

But no. I couldn't log in to the account and kept getting emails saying I still owed the fee. After numerous phone calls, they finally realised they hadn't linked my sister's payment to my account. They had to delete and redo my account, but finally, at noon on Friday, I got my membership. I informed work, and thankfully, I could start on Monday. Talk about last-minute stress.

Interestingly, throughout this whole ordeal, I was strangely calm. I was out on a run when I received the email saying the payment had yet to go through. I made the necessary phone calls and did what I could, but beyond that, it was out of my control.

I'm not always this calm under pressure, but I'm working on it. I'm learning to focus on what I can control and not stress (too much) about what I can't. It's an ongoing process and a life lesson I'm still mastering. Earlier in life, I needed to voice my thoughts immediately, but now I realise that sometimes it's better to wait, think things through, and respond later. Sometimes, the best response is just a smile or nothing at all. Going for a run instead of reacting negatively has helped me grow more than ever imagined.

**Doubts**
What have I done? Is this the right move? Is this the best for my family and my career?

I'll go through these phases, especially as I settle in. I keep reminding myself that once work falls into a routine, I join running groups, make friends, and get my family over here, things will settle. I'm making a point to enjoy the process—to explore, to adapt, and to be present.

But I need help with doubts about running the 100 miler. Is it normal to feel this way, even without all the other changes I've gone through? I went out for a 20 km run but felt so flat and tired. At the same time, I realise I need to give myself grace. My body and mind are going through massive changes, not to mention having just completed the Comrades Ultra. I need to continue believing in myself and my training, to trust in my stubborn nature that drives me to pursue enormous goals and work hard to achieve them. I've done regular, consistent exercise and the best preparation possible. And most importantly, I have immense support from friends and family who believe in me. The rest is up to race day.

I turned to social media to share my thoughts and ask for advice. It's been a place—especially on Facebook—where I've learned much from friends who have regularly completed 100-mile races. What I've loved most is seeing the same advice echoed in the comments:

- Run your race.
- Prepare mentally.
- Plan your race.
- Eat every hour.
- Stop to appreciate your surroundings.
- Smile at a fellow athlete.

It's not just about the physical training; massive mental preparedness is needed, too. And then there's the gear—testing it out, ensuring it's right. A great support crew is essential, even just for a hug and a few encouraging words to keep you going. All these little things add up to make an enormous adventure. Ultra running is a team sport—I've heard this from newbies to experienced pros. Ultimately, it's one foot in front of the other—keep going.

## Adapting to London

Glen and I lived in the UK from 2006 to 2011, and we were in London for the first few months. I thought I understood how to get around on the underground and public transport and the general workings of a major city. Or so I thought. Fast forward a few years, and despite considerable effort to obtain pounds in cash before I left—which I managed to do—cash is useless! I couldn't even buy a coffee with cash; they didn't care and would rather lose the sale. This is wild! Where I'm from, cash is king, and now I have a lot of useless cash that I can't deposit into my bank because I'm still waiting for my new bank card to arrive. Sigh.

The most significant change in London since COVID-19 is how so many companies now have their employees working remotely, which saves on travel and allows them to continue working. Anything that could minimise germ transfer was embraced, like not passing cash from person to person. At least I could use some of it to top up my Oyster card for transport...and then I learned that Oyster cards are also archaic. Everyone now uses their phone or bank card with the tap function. Again, there is no card and no active bank account. It's all a lot to adapt to, but I'm learning one step at a time.

## Charlton Parkrun

As a warm-up, I arrived at Charlton Parkrun using the jog from where I was staying. It was a beautiful, sunny day with just the right temperature. As I arrived early, a giant birthday sign greeted me—Charlton Parkrun was celebrating its first anniversary that morning. Charlton Park is a beautiful open field with three loops of the 5 km route. In the UK, parkruns start promptly at 9 am on Saturday mornings. A buzz was in the air as people warmed up, stretched, and got ready to start. Newcomers were invited to a separate area five minutes before the beginning, where we were briefed on how the parkrun worked, with its three laps leading to the finish.

I didn't know anyone and kept to myself. I decided to start mid-pack to see how things felt and figured I could always push harder if needed. We ran the circumference of the main field, then crossed a small path to a second adjoining field to complete our first lap. There was plenty of space to overtake runners, and the competition was intense. I decided to give it my all. After the first lap, I increased my pace, and in the final lap, I managed to pass another lady to finish first in my age category. Completely out of breath, I congratulated the lady behind me and began conversing. Her name was Peppa, and she lived in the area. Her husband was marshalling that morning with their young son in tow. We chatted away, and I felt utterly refreshed to have met someone and spent time with them afterwards.

Parkruns are a fantastic way to test your speed, get pushed by others, and measure your progress if you repeat the same course later. I felt invigorated to have made a new friend. This was a great speed session for me, and although I had planned to do some others, I focused on races leading up to my 100 miler. When I arrived in the UK, finding a rhythm with regular runs, like parkrun or other races, was essential to keep me focused during those last eight weeks. I was thankful for the races I did and for joining London City Runners for their weekly Wednesday track sessions.

## London City Runners (LCR)

When I landed in London, I began investigating where to find a hill to train on, but this was a challenging task. London doesn't have the kind of inclines needed for severe elevation training. The best suggestions were Greenwich Park in the East and Box Hill far to the southwest. Greenwich was relatively nearby, but Box Hill was logistically too far to train on regularly. At a loss for hill training, I adopted some speed training instead. The idea was to push my body and mind even when tired, increase my leg strength, and work on other cardio systems. I made the best of what I had available.

The Wednesday evening track sessions were convenient with LCR, with coaches and other runners pushing me to do better in a structured program. The sessions were well-organised, with runners grouped based on their 5 km time. We'd start with a group dynamic warm-up, explain the evening track session, and divide into our groups. This system worked well, as you were always pushed within your group and could aim to push further by keeping up with the runners ahead of you. I learned a lot and found these sessions helped me focus, provided a weekly routine, and introduced me to some fantastic people. The evenings were perfectly crisp, with only a light jacket needed to start. After the sessions, I would cool down by running to the train station through the park.

I desperately sought races to encourage me to complete longer distances and keep me motivated in the weeks leading up to my 100 miler. I didn't want to travel far or spend a fortune, nor did I want to spend an entire weekend travelling for one race. Thankfully, I found two races nearby on dates that worked for me.

**Pure Sports Medicine**

My first work week was a whirlwind as I slowly got into the flow of things. I left the house on Tuesday morning at 6:40 am to catch the Dockland Light Rail (DLR) to Bank in central London. With train strikes planned for the following day, I decided to familiarise myself with the DLR route instead of the Elizabeth tube line. These train strikes have been a regular occurrence for over a year, causing frustration for many as they disrupt central London by preventing commuters from reaching their jobs. Fortunately, we usually receive a few weeks' notice about the strike action, including the affected lines and expected disruptions. While the underground is rarely fully affected, certain train companies come to a complete standstill on strike days, operating with reduced hours and starting much later than usual. This creates chaos, and careful planning is needed to navigate around it. I'm grateful that my workplace is understanding, especially since there are often no viable alternatives if you live far away.

With my mind in overdrive, planning for the next 24 hours, I packed the night before, including a set of running clothes and lunch. I prefer making my lunch as much as possible—it saves a small fortune and is often the healthier option with a bit of planning.

The workday was filled with administrative tasks, meeting colleagues, and excitement about implementing new ideas in my Head of Rehab (HOR) role. The following day would be my first in this role, where I would visit all seven clinics, meet the teams, and offer support. I love the dual nature of my job—I'm a clinician, treating patients three days a week, and a HOR for the remaining two, focusing on admin and team support across the clinics. I see my role as the glue that interlinks the rehab team, supporting them in their roles, encouraging their best performance, and helping them develop through continuous professional and personal growth.

I had researched running clubs in the London area, and London City Runners (LCR) kept popping up as the most popular. Based in central London, they have three regular evening runs. Tuesday and Thursday evenings are along the Thames, while Wednesday evenings are dedicated track sessions at the Southwark Park Athletics Track, which must be booked in advance.

Straight after work, I ran to the LCR hub in the heart of the Bermondsey Beer Mile. There are several starting times, with specific routes that can be easily shortened or lengthened depending on your ability or the distance you want to run. If you're new to the club, you can either stick with a runner of similar pace or look up the routes beforehand—they're straightforward—and go for it. Everyone sets off at their own pace, meeting back at the club afterwards for a catch-up and a drink.

I left with the 18:15 group, and London was bustling with commuters by this time. Dodging the crowds and keeping up with the group was challenging, but I continued along the Thames path. The route is simple, but it occasionally throws a curveball, where you must veer away from the Thames before rejoining the path. The night sky was alive with music, festivities, and the bright colours of the London Eye. I kept pace with my fellow LCR runners and made it back, feeling a bit pushed but enjoying the flat terrain.

Knowing I still had the journey home ahead of me, I didn't stay long. I headed back to the DLR for the return trip to Woolwich Arsenal, grabbed some food from the local shop, and walked through the door at 21:35. In time to wolf down some dinner, pack for the next workday, and finally collapse into bed by 23:00.

The week flew by in a whirlwind of patients, admin tasks, meeting more of the team, and slowly adapting to the bustling London lifestyle—complete with its elegant coffee choices. The latter was essential in my integration into London life, almost like a rite of passage.

However, my well-laid plans hit an unexpected speed bump thanks to the ongoing train strikes. I floundered late into the night, trying to figure out the best way to get to the Spartan Race I had eagerly booked for Saturday morning. The clock showed 12:37 am on Friday, well past midnight, and I had already spent three to four hours, if not longer, searching for transport options. The train strike had thrown everything into chaos, and the prices for alternatives were absurdly high despite the myriad options I had explored.

With much frustration and significant help from my host, John, we figured out a workaround. I could catch a train on Friday evening—while they were still running—and stay overnight nearby, then take an Uber to the race start in the morning. Determined not to miss the Spartan Race, which I had heard so much about and saw as excellent training for my 100 miler, I decided to go for it. I hit "enter" and booked my ticket, only to panic when I thought I'd booked for the wrong day. After a tense few seconds, I realised that my tired brain had overlooked that it was already Friday, not Thursday. To top it off, I misplaced my bank card between the downstairs and upstairs of the house. After a frantic search—and a few choice words—I found it tucked away inside my closed laptop.

Putting things into perspective, this was the end of my first whole week of work and living in London. I had landed just eight days earlier and secured accommodation, navigated the various transport systems (with a steep learning curve for the most valuable apps), regularly fed myself, and found running groups and races to keep me motivated. It had been a hectic first week, filled with excitement, little sleep, and an overwhelming amount of planning.

I was grateful that, for now, it was just myself I had to look after and not my family. Although I missed them, it was easier to manage my schedule, fitting things in at the last minute without the need to plan meals or worry about anyone else. I made time to explore my surroundings, familiarise myself with the area, and fully immerse myself in work. The weather was gloriously mild for October, although the darker mornings and evenings hinted at the impending winter chill.

I thrive on organising, planning, and setting goals, so having running events lined up helped me stay balanced and focused, diverting my attention from missing friends and family. My workdays, thankfully, weren't too hectic as I settled in, allowing me to ease into an entirely different, digital-first environment gently. I had moved from a paper-filled process to a fully online system, which required me to learn many protocols and programs to do my job effectively. I paced myself, knowing that adapting would take time.

Despite the busy and exciting start, a nagging concern loomed over me: finding accommodation for my family when I returned in January. Although it was still early, there were few options available. I needed to find a place with a manageable commute to London, good schools, affordability, and, crucially, one that would accept Storm, our border collie. This search was at the forefront of my mind, adding a layer of stress to an otherwise exhilarating new chapter in my life.

### Spartan London South East European Champs, Pippingford Park, Kent

The Spartan London South East European Championship at Pippingford Park, Kent, was an event that genuinely lived up to its reputation for both the challenges and the atmosphere it offered. Spartan races are known for their mix of intense competition and fun, and this event was no different. From the moment I arrived, the buzz of anticipation was palpable.

Thanks to my obstacle course-loving friend, Julia, I first heard about Spartan races in South Africa. She had completed a Trifecta weekend—three Spartan races of different distances in one weekend—and showed me her impressive collection of medals. Her enthusiasm was contagious, and soon after, I joined her for a taster session. Despite running fit, I quickly realised I lacked the strength and balance needed for obstacles. It was a humbling experience, but it sparked a passion in me. Over time, I began attending obstacle training sessions, slowly improving my abilities. Another friend, Andre, had told me about the spear throw, a Spartan-specific obstacle that intrigued me even more.

This Spartan race would be my first obstacle course event, not just any race— it was the European Championship, which added excitement and competition. I had signed up for the Beast distance, a gruelling 21 km course with 32 obstacles. Knowing it was my first time, I started with the open group and opted for a mid-morning start in case of any transportation issues getting to the venue.

The days leading up to the event were filled with preparation. I watched YouTube videos, researched the obstacles I might face, and asked experienced racers for advice. Still, I knew that much of it would come down to how I handled the barriers on the day. My excitement was mixed with nerves, but I was determined to give it my all. After a busy workday on Friday, I made my way to the train station with all my gear for the weekend. I had booked a hotel near the venue, about a 40-minute walk from the station. As I arrived at the hotel, a light rain began to fall—welcome to the unpredictability of British weather! I checked in, sorted out my room, and booked an Uber for the following day to ensure I arrived at the race venue with plenty of time to spare. The room was simple but comfortable, with all the essentials, and I managed to fall asleep quickly despite my excitement.

Morning came too soon, and I jumped out of bed, eager to start the day. As I boiled the kettle for a much-needed cup of tea, a screeching alarm and flashing red lights suddenly filled the room. Panic set in as I realised the steam from the kettle had triggered the fire alarm. I quickly turned it off, flung open the door to let the steam escape, and hoped that I wouldn't be the one to blame for waking everyone up. Fortunately, the alarms went off in every room, so I wasn't alone in trying to stop the noise.

With that bit of early morning drama behind me, I gathered my belongings, hopped into the waiting Uber, and made my way through the winding country roads of south Kent to Pippingford Park.

Arriving at the venue, I was struck by the event's sheer size. Even though it was still early, the parking field was already filling up, and energising music drifted across the venue. The atmosphere was electric, and as I walked down to the registration area, I couldn't resist taking some pictures of the Spartan fanatics and their decked-out vehicles. The sun was shining, and felt like the perfect day for a race.

Registration was straightforward. After showing my ID, I received my Spartan bandana with my race number and a hearty "Aroo!" from the volunteers. I dropped off my bags at the bag check and took a moment to soak in the scene. The Spartan décor was impressive, and I couldn't resist taking a few more selfies in front of the massive Spartan logos.

With some time before my start, I watched the earlier waves of racers set off, led by the legendary Spartan Phil, who was dressed head-to-toe in Spartan gear. His pre-race speech was motivational and interactive, reminding us that we were all Spartans and that today was our day to seek glory. The energy was infectious, and I felt ready to take on whatever challenges the course had in store for me. Aroo!

As the time for my batch drew nearer, I could feel the nerves kicking in. Finally, it was our turn to enter the start pen. The energy was palpable as bodies jostled into position, and Spartan Phil's voice boomed out the first question, "Who are the Spartan virgins?" Half of our group raised their hands, including me. The music met it's crescendo, signalling that it was time. With his infectious enthusiasm, Spartan Phil gave us the final encouragement, and we were off!

I had positioned myself near the front of the pack, knowing that the first part of the course was a running section. I wanted to avoid getting caught in the crowd and losing momentum. We zigzagged across a field, and before long, we reached our first obstacle: four hurdles. My adrenaline was pumping, and I cleared them without much trouble. The next challenge was the balance beam. I could already see a fellow Spartan off to the side, completing his penalty burpees, having failed the obstacle.

The sight only added to the pressure, but I was determined not to falter so early in the race.

The balance beam tested my focus and nerves, especially with people lining up behind me. The pressure was on, but I crossed with a leap at the end, avoiding a fall. Back to running, I caught sight of the following obstacles looming ahead: over and under walls, a vertical cargo net, and then the dreaded Ape Hanger—a series of widely spaced bars requiring a solid swing to navigate. I had practised similar obstacles in training, but nothing prepared me for the real thing. I swung from bar to bar, feeling the strain on my arms and shoulders. I lost my grip and slipped as I reached for the final bar. Gutted, I trudged to the penalty loop, frustrated but determined to keep going.

One of the significant aspects of Spartan races is the opportunity to watch others tackle the obstacles. It's both inspiring and educational. Watching others, I could see different techniques and strategies, which I mentally stored away for the next time. Spartan obstacles require a mix of strength, confidence, and technique. The more you practise under different conditions, the more efficient and confident you become. I was still very much a novice, learning to balance all three.

I found the walls and climbing nets manageable. However, hanging obstacles and heavy lifts, like the Herc Hoist, were more challenging. The Herc Hoist, in particular, was tough because it came towards the end of the race when fatigue had set in. It's an obstacle that involves hoisting a heavy weight up using a rope, and while I completed it, it required every ounce of energy I had left.

Some obstacles, such as the Atlas Carry, are modified with different weights for men and women. I was thrilled to complete this one successfully—picking up a heavy concrete ball and carrying it a set distance before putting it down without crushing my toes. The sandbag carry was another weighted obstacle, with different bags for men and women. I found it manageable, though I didn't run with it, opting instead to focus on maintaining a steady pace. I experimented with different ways of carrying the bag—over my shoulder, in one arm, against my chest—each method offering slight relief to other muscle groups.

The venue at Pippingford Park was stunningly hilly, which played to my strengths. I relished the trail running sections, powering up the hills and flying down the descents—the combination of obstacles and the natural terrain made for a challenging but exhilarating race.

As I continued the course, I encountered a mix of successes and struggles. Some obstacles I conquered with relative ease, while others left me breathless and battling. Each challenge was a learning experience, and I knew I could improve with more training and experience. The Spartan race was everything I had hoped for—demanding, exciting, and fun. It was an incredible introduction to the world of obstacle course racing, and I left the course feeling both accomplished and eager for the next challenge.

The Spartan Beast race at Pippingford Park had been a rollercoaster of challenges and triumphs, and one of the obstacles that loomed large in my mind before the race even started was the swim. The thought of swimming across a small, icy lake fully clothed in my gear was daunting. The cold water and the added weight of my shoes made it seem even more formidable. The safety measures in place gave me the confidence to try: a rope on the side of the lake to hold onto and two canoeists ready to assist if needed.

As soon as I stepped into the water, the ground disappeared beneath my feet, and I was fully submerged. The icy chill took my breath away, and the weight of my shoes made swimming difficult. But I forced myself to remain calm, checked that I could still breathe, and slowly began to walk across the lake, sticking close to the rope for security. I'm not the best swimmer on a good day, and this was far from ideal conditions. Still, I persevered and completed the swim, to my great relief. This one made me the proudest of all the obstacles in the race. I had promised myself that I would at least try every obstacle, and overcoming the swim felt like a significant victory.

Another memorable obstacle was the Tyrolean traverse, a 20-foot rope suspended above water that participants must cross while hanging upside down. Thanks to my training, I was comfortable with this technique— alternating between pulling with my arms and legs as I inched along the rope. Long socks or tights were essential here to prevent rope burn on the shins as I slid across. At one point, I became a bit overconfident, and my leg slipped, leaving me hanging solely by my arms. I had to quickly pull myself up and re-hook my leg onto the rope. They reminded me not to underestimate any obstacle, no matter how comfortable I was.

The Beater monkey bars, however, proved to be my nemesis. They consist of monkey bars with a twisting beater section that rotates, adding a new difficulty level. I watched a few people attempt it, but I couldn't quite wrap my mind around how to transfer onto the rotating section and continue. Despite my best efforts, I dropped down and had to take on the penalty loop. It indicated that I needed more practice on this type of obstacle for next time.

The spear throw was another iconic obstacle I was eager to try. I watched a couple of competitors as they nailed their throws, making it look almost effortless. I carefully ensured the rope wasn't twisted, took aim, and threw with all my might. Unfortunately, I overthrew the target, and the spear sailed past its mark. It's another penalty loop for me. I realised that the spear throw required more precision than power, and while I missed the mark this time, it was my first attempt, so I wasn't too disappointed.

As the race neared, I faced the multi-rig, a daunting obstacle with various hanging elements. Given my earlier struggles, especially with the Beater, I was determined to give this one my all. I confidently navigated the monkey bars and other grips, but the final challenge was two short ropes before the bell that signalled completion. I made it to the end but hesitated. Could I swing without using the last two ropes? I decided to go for it but missed the rope and fell, leading to another penalty loop. Despite this, I was thrilled to have made it so far and proud of the effort I'd put in.

Finally, I approached the last obstacle: the inverted wall. With one final burst of energy, I scrambled over it and headed towards the finish line, where the iconic fire jump awaited. Leaping over the flames, I crossed the finish line, exhilarated and exhausted. The feeling of accomplishment was overwhelming as I was awarded a flashy Spartan medal and collected my finisher's shirt.

I had completed the Spartan Beast—22 kilometres in 2 hours and 51 minutes, with 817 metres of elevation. The race had pushed me to my limits, but I had risen to the challenge. Each obstacle taught me something new, and I left the event with a sense of pride and a hunger to improve for the next one. The experience solidified my love for obstacle course racing and reminded me why pushing through fear and discomfort is always worth it.

The exhilaration after crossing the finish line of the Spartan Beast was palpable. I was still feeling adrenaline as I walked through the event area, looking for Megan, whom I had "met" through our mutual friend James from obstacle training. We planned to meet after the race, and I was grateful when she kindly offered to give me a lift to Tunbridge Wells. We chatted briefly, sharing our race experiences, but it lasted only briefly as Megan and her crew were gearing up for another race the following day.

The weather was on our side—beautifully sunny, though still in the cool mid-teens. With my bags in hand, I headed towards the train station, expecting a smooth journey home. However, upon arrival, I was greeted by massive signs declaring that no trains were operating due to the ongoing train strikes. Usually, this would have sent me into a panic, but since moving to the UK, I've tried to adapt to the unexpected with more grace. I could not do anything about the strikes, so I immediately switched to problem-solving mode.

## Plan B and B

A quick check on Google confirmed my fears: no public transport options were available, and even Uber was outrageously expensive and unavailable. With my options narrowing, I turned to finding accommodation for the night. Fortunately, a quick search led me to a lovely bed and breakfast just a 20-minute walk from town. I booked a room, grateful to have found a solution, and made my way there.

The B&B was a stately, comfortable place, providing the perfect respite after the day's exertions. I was relieved to drop off my bags and leisurely walk around the estate. The late afternoon sun was beginning to dip, and the fatigue from the race and the last-minute changes began to set in. It was a moment to reflect and unwind. The following day, breakfast was nothing short of divine— both a continental spread and a full English breakfast awaited, and I indulged in both, knowing I had earned it. Feeling well-fed and content, I left the B&B just after 9 am and returned to the train station. Although the strikes weren't in full swing that day, reduced services meant that many trains still weren't running, and bus replacements were the only option. My journey home was slow, taking up half the day, but I finally walked through my front door just after 2 pm, exhausted and accomplished.

Once home, I decided to check the Spartan results online, not expecting much but curious nonetheless. To my great surprise and delight, I discovered I had placed fourth overall among the women in the open group, first in my age category, and 65th out of 1,060 participants. The news was the perfect capstone to an already memorable experience. Despite the unexpected challenges, the whole adventure had been an incredible physical and mental experience. It was a fantastic test run for my upcoming 100 miler, reinforcing the importance of flexibility, resilience, and a positive mindset. And with the seed now sown, I'm eager to push for even more in the next race.

## Camino Epping Forest 50 km

The workweek flew by in a blur of meetings, appointments, and the ever-present hum of administration. Still, when the weekend rolled around, I eagerly anticipated the Camino Epping Forest 50 km trail run. I had heard fantastic things about Epping Forest—the beauty, the serenity, and the lush green landscapes—so I was excited to experience it firsthand, even more so because it was conveniently accessible by public transport.

When I signed up for the race, the organisers mentioned that road shoes might suffice unless the weather turns, in which case there could be some muddy patches. This left me a bit puzzled—this was supposed to be a trail race, typically involving uneven terrain. Nevertheless, I decided to stick with my trusty trail shoes, figuring they'd serve me well regardless of the conditions.

On the morning of the race, I set out early, as I often do, with Google Maps as my guide. The cool air was refreshing, and I was eager to get to the start line. However, after about ten minutes of walking, I realised I needed to head in a different direction. It's always unsettling when this happens, but I had plenty of time to correct course, so I turned around and soon began to spot other runners heading in the same direction. It felt a bit strange, though, as we moved deeper into a residential area rather than the wilds of a forest.

Finally, after recalibrating my sense of direction, I found myself in the company of other runners, all making their way towards a large open field near a pub, which served as the start line. As I arrived, I drew a few curious looks, my running vest stuffed to the brim with gear, including my poles. While some runners looked surprised, others bravely asked whether the course had steep hills requiring such equipment. I explained that this race was a trial run for my upcoming 100-miler, and I wanted to get used to carrying everything I'd need on race day.

The morning was perfect—a crisp chill in the air, the sun just beginning to peek through, and a dense fog covering the field, giving the scene a magical, almost otherworldly feel. It was the kind of weather that made you feel at home, no matter where you were. As the start time approached, the runners' energy buzz grew palpable. Last-minute toilet trips were made, kits were checked and rechecked, and a collective sense of excitement filled the air.

**This was the start of something special.**

Coming from Durban, where the trail running community is tight-knit and familiar, the Epping Forest, 50 km race brought back memories of when I first started trail running—when I didn't know anyone, and everything felt new. Many runners seemed to know each other, greeting one another like old friends, while I felt like an outsider. I tried to converse with a few fellow runners, but it felt more like they were being polite rather than genuinely interested. Feeling disheartened, I decided to take some solo pictures and keep to myself.

These moments of loneliness hit hard. I couldn't help but think of my friends in Durban, with whom I'd shared countless hours of training and racing. Now, I was starting from scratch in this new environment, and it wasn't easy. London might offer glittering new opportunities, but there's also the reality of rebuilding your social circle and finding your place in a new community. It's a reminder that there's also the challenge of starting over beneath the surface of excitement and novelty.

Thankfully, the feeling didn't linger long. The organisers called us together for the final instructions, and before I knew it, we were off. I set off at a moderate pace, sticking to the middle of the pack, cautious not to overdo it too early, especially since I was unfamiliar with the terrain. As I ran, I found solace in the rhythm of my steps and the soft music playing in the background. The flat, beautiful terrain of Epping Forest and the cool weather made for an enjoyable run. Although I had anticipated a more rugged trail, the hard-packed paths were well-suited for road shoes. I chuckled at my decision to wear trail shoes, but it was all part of the learning experience.

The course was straightforward—a marked out-and-back route through the forest. Along the way, we were greeted by the friendliest aid stations, offering an array of snacks from fruit to chocolate and gels. The volunteers cheered us on, making us feel like winners at every stop. As I approached the latter part of the race, I found myself craving a hill, even a small one, to justify a walk. This is the trail runner in me. Years ago, as a road runner, the thought of walking during a run would have horrified me, but trail running has taught me the value of pacing and the necessity of walking, especially in ultra-distance races. I found a poor excuse for a hill and indulged in a brief speed walk, though I felt a twinge of guilt for not pushing through.

After self-talk, I resolved to run the final 10 km no matter what. The pace didn't matter as much as the commitment to keep moving. I treated it as mental training for my 100-miler. When I hit 40 km, I was tired and a bit grumpy, but I stuck to my plan. Once green and inviting, the forest became a tunnel I just wanted to get through. Eventually, the trees gave way to fields, and I spotted the finish arch in the distance. I picked up the pace, determined to finish strong. After the mandatory finish line photo with a jump, I received my race patch, grabbed a coffee, and collapsed on the grass to watch other runners finish. I clocked in just over 5 hours, which I was content with, though a part of me couldn't help but think I could have shaved off a few minutes to achieve a sub-5-hour finish. That competitive spirit never entirely goes away.

This race was more than just a physical challenge; it was a mental exercise in resilience and adaptation. It reminded me that starting over, whether in running or life, is never easy, but you eventually find your stride with time, patience, and perseverance.

I slowly began to understand one of the significant differences in terminology and expectations regarding running in the UK. The word "trail" here didn't quite align with what I had always known it to be. In the UK, particularly in the south, a trail could mean a grassy or patched park, off-road grass, or firm ground. Still, it often needed more technical challenges I associated with trail running back in South Africa. The terrain was generally smoother, with fewer steep sections or rocky paths. I discovered that what I had always considered "trail running" was more akin to what the British call "fell running." Fell running involves technical trails, uneven ground, steep sections, and a race director who doesn't necessarily need to warn you about every bump or hole on the course—something that would be marked with luminous tape and orange beacons in a UK trail race.

Despite these differences, I was grateful to have completed the 50 km race as my long run. It was a valuable lesson in persistence, especially during the last 10 km when I wanted to walk more than I did. This experience reaffirmed something that I had been increasingly learning during my time in London: mileage training, while important, is just one piece of the puzzle. The mental aspect of running—developing resilience, pushing through discomfort, and maintaining focus—is even more crucial, especially when preparing for an ultra-distance event like the 100-miler.

Given the limitations of my current environment—where gaining elevation and finding truly technical terrain were challenges—I chose to focus on strengthening my mind and mental toughness. I realised that while I couldn't replicate the exact physical conditions I would face in my 100-miler, I could prepare myself mentally to tackle whatever came my way. This shift in focus was a significant part of my training in London, and it taught me the importance of adaptability and resilience in the face of new and unexpected challenges.

**London living**

Living in London has been a whirlwind of adjustment, discovery, and a fair amount of admin. For anyone moving to a new country, particularly one like the UK, the sheer amount of bureaucratic hoops can be overwhelming. It often feels like a game of "which comes first," where you need A to get B, but frustratingly, B is required to get A. Thankfully, I had some prior experience, having lived in the UK from 2006 to 2011. I already had a bank account and a National Insurance number, but with my bank card expired, even seemingly simple tasks required time and patience.

I've learned that in situations like these, prioritisation is critical. I needed to focus on the most urgent tasks, ticking them off individually. As I was also preparing for a significant race, ensuring I got plenty of rest and a balanced diet became crucial—both to keep my training on track and avoid getting sick.

Here are some London essentials that I've picked up along the way:

- **Google Maps**: An absolute lifesaver! The public transport feature is indispensable for planning routes and timing your travel. The live coverage is fantastic, especially when you're on a bus, as it tells you how many stops are left and where exactly you are—quite an upgrade from 2011!

- **National Rail Card**: If you're travelling within Southeast London, invest in a National Rail Card. It costs £30 a year, but you save a third on travel costs, and it can include up to four people.

- **The Trainline App** is another great planning tool for buying tickets directly. It simplifies travelling around London and beyond.

- **Shop Apps**: Download the apps for your favourite shops before shopping. It saves time and money, and you gain rewards in the long run.

- **Good Earphones**: In London, a good set of earphones is essential. If you travel on the underground regularly, noise-cancelling earphones are a good investment. However, if you prefer to stay aware of your surroundings while running, Shokz's bone-conducting technology is fantastic—comfortable, rechargeable, and with a long battery life.

- **Spare Clothes**: Always pack spare clothes, especially underwear, when travelling. With frequent train strikes, you never know when you might be stuck somewhere, and having something clean to change into can make all the difference.

- **Cash**: Surprisingly, money is not useful in London. Often, you'll pay extra if you use it, places don't accept it, or they don't have change. It's best to rely on bank cards or mobile payment methods.

- **Oyster Card**: While initially helpful, Oyster cards are rapidly becoming outdated. Most people now use their bank cards, watches or buy tickets directly.

- **Navigating Crowds**: In London, being jostled, pushed, and squeezed is normal, and no one apologises. Walk confidently in your chosen direction, avoid zigzagging, and stay focused to avoid bumping into people or accidentally slowing down.

- **Train Strikes**: Always check for planned train closures or strikes in advance so you can plan accordingly. Train strikes have been ongoing for over a year, and there's no sign of them stopping soon.

- **Comfortable Shoes**: Comfort is critical when commuting in London. While you might want to wear fancy shoes, most Londoners opt for trainers or running shoes, even with their smart clothes. They'll change into formal shoes once they get to work—commutable comfort is the priority.

While walking around the bank area one day, I noticed a long queue outside an eatery, and many other nearby places had no line. It struck me as amusing that Londoners, who will loudly complain about a train being two minutes late, are perfectly willing to wait twenty minutes or more for lunch. This place was exceptional—I might have to queue up one day to see the fuss.

There's nothing quite as stressful as feeling like you're the source of frustration for a crowd of hurried London commuters. I've managed to experience this several times, thanks to my bank app's infuriatingly temperamental behaviour. Picture this: I'm underground, ready to tap and go, only for the app to fail at a crucial moment. I try again, by which time a small crowd of three to five people has already gathered behind me, all impatiently waiting for me to get out of the way. Embarrassed, I step aside, fiddling with my phone, trying to get the app to cooperate. Finally, after yet another rejection, I dig into my bag, pull out my bank card, and tap the machine, which promptly beeps and lets me through. The whole ordeal is not only frustrating but mortifying. I eventually learned to have the app loaded and open before tapping, but honestly, it became easier to use my actual bank card, especially since I don't use the underground regularly.

Lidl has quickly become one of my go-to grocery shops. It's reasonably priced, offers a variety of foods, and always has some fun non-food items to browse. However, my routine grocery shopping trips haven't been without their mishaps. One evening, close to closing time, the shop was bustling, and I headed to the self-checkout with my basket. As I was scanning my items, I reached for the eggs. I thought I was careful, but as I placed them in the bagging area, the container somehow opened, sending eggs smashing over half my groceries, the self-checkout machine, and the floor. I was mortified. I didn't even know where to start cleaning up the mess.

Thankfully, one of the shop assistants quickly came to my rescue. She kindly helped clean up the disaster and suggested I get another carton of eggs. At that moment, I couldn't deal with the situation any longer. I left the eggs behind, scanned the rest of my groceries, and exited the shop. The faster I could get out, the better. Even though it was an honest mistake, I felt tiny, like all eyes were on me, judging me for holding up the till and causing further delays. While stressful and embarrassing, these little mishaps are all part of the adjustment process. They serve as small reminders that no matter how much we try to blend in and keep things running smoothly, sometimes life has other plans, and all we can do is roll with it, learn from it, and hopefully, laugh about it later.

**Finding home**

The small things, the seemingly inconsequential details, often carry the most weight when you're adapting to a new life in a different country. It's surprising how a simple issue, like a hair straightener not working, can catalyse a wave of emotions. Something so minor can unravel your sense of preparedness, instantly making you feel completely out of sorts. I nearly cried over this minor setback, which highlighted how small, everyday obstacles can pile up and feel overwhelming.

Moving countries isn't just about the big tasks, like buying plane tickets or packing up your life. Those are straightforward in comparison. The real challenges are the things you might not even think about until they're right in front of you—like figuring out mobile phone contracts, navigating public transport, finding familiar brands in the shops, and realising that cash is rarely accepted here. Yet, your bank account access is still pending. It's about remembering to bring an extra bag for shopping, planning meals and exercise around your workday, and figuring out how to manage without the conveniences you're used to.

Despite these hurdles, things do get easier. Each little victory, like finally getting that straightener to work or finding your way through the maze of London's public transport, is significant. Recognising these small wins, celebrating them, and knowing they'll add up over time is crucial. The transition is tough, but it's important to remember that every little accomplishment is a step towards feeling more settled. One of my most significant stressors has been securing a home for our family. The rental market in and around London is incredibly competitive right now, mainly due to the ongoing effects of COVID-19, with more people commuting into London and driving up both prices and demand in commuter towns. Finding a suitable home that we could afford, with good schools nearby, has been daunting.

I started my search in the southern parts of London based on recommendations from colleagues and friends. The cost was a significant factor, but I also wanted to ensure the commute into central London would be manageable—ideally under an hour. I used OpenRent, a fantastic platform where you deal directly with property owners while still having the security and checks of an agency. After scouring listings and finding a few options within our budget, I finally came across a beautiful home in Sevenoaks, Kent, just outside the M25.

I was getting a viewing, and it felt like a significant victory. I planned my journey carefully, arriving early to get a feel for the town. Sevenoaks greeted me with a perfect autumn day—bright skies and crisp air, a welcome change from the hustle of London. As I explored, I saw a friendly, active community: runners, dog walkers, and an outdoor women's exercise class. The town centre was bustling, and I even indulged in homemade treats at the local market. I continued towards the house, taking my time to explore. I passed local tennis clubs potential running routes and even stumbled upon a running shop where I struck up a conversation with a local runner. He shared insights about the area, pointing out the many open spaces like Knole Park and the North Downs, which are perfect for long runs. The town felt vibrant yet calm, with its theatre, numerous wedding shops, and even live music playing in the streets.

Walking through Sevenoaks was a breath of fresh air after the intensity of London. The slower pace, the friendly faces, and the sense of community were exactly what I was hoping to find. It was a stark contrast to London, where people often keep to themselves, heads down, earphones in. Here, people made eye contact and greeted you, and there was a general warmth in the air. Finding this home felt like a significant step towards settling in for me and my family. It's a place where we can put down roots, where Glen can enjoy tennis, and where I can continue running, all while being close enough to London to manage the daily commute. It's a reminder that while adapting to a new country can be challenging, it's also full of big and small discoveries that make it all worthwhile.

I've always held a particular Bible verse close to my heart: "Whatever you do, work at it with all your heart, as working for the Lord, not for men," from Colossians 3:23. It's been a guiding principle through high school exams and every challenge I've taken on. I set high standards for myself, but having friends and family to keep me grounded has been a blessing. They help me maintain perspective, especially when I get caught up in striving for perfection.

## My "why"

Soon, I'll be in the midst of my 100-mile dream. It's a daunting challenge, but why did I enter this race? What makes it so unique? The significance goes beyond the sheer scale of the event. Yes, it's a colossal, gruelling trail race with rough terrain and massive elevation, but it holds an even deeper meaning for me. It felt like a major setback when I detached my hamstring in 2019. However, the surgeon reassured me that I could return to running without restriction with the proper rehabilitation, patience, and persistence. Since then, I've wanted to show you can still dream big after a setback. This race is about proving that anything is possible with the right mindset and hard work. It's a testament to the journey of starting with that first step and building towards something extraordinary.

This race is for my Wander Women to show that a journey of 100 miles begins with just one step. It's for the working moms out there, trying to balance work, marriage, and children, often feeling like they're not getting it right but still pushing on. I get it—I'm right there with them.

And it's for me. This race terrifies me as much as it excites me, but that makes it so meaningful. I have an incredible team of friends and family supporting me physically, emotionally, and from afar. I love every part of the process—the planning, the training, the mental preparation, and the careful gear selection. Despite appearances, ultras are not a solo endeavour; they're very much a team sport. People often ask what considerable distances I've tackled before this. My longest trail run was the 13 Peaks Challenge—110 kilometres on the same terrain, with no sleep but lots of laughter and Krispy Kreme doughnuts to keep us going.

Before moving to the UK, I had meticulously planned my training schedule. I would run the Comrades Marathon, take a brief break, and then ramp up my training, particularly on elevation work, in preparation for the 100-miler. But life had other plans, and I couldn't say no when an incredible career opportunity in London came up. This sudden change meant last-minute packing and replanning, but I was determined to keep my training on track. One major challenge presented itself: London is flat, and technical trails take time to come by. I quickly researched local trail races, obstacle courses, and road races, signing up for what I could find. The Spartan and Camino Epping 50 km forest races seemed like good options, so I went for them.

These past three weeks have been harsh. Some days, I haven't wanted to do anything. I've been wrestling with learning new work programs, understanding my role, meeting new people, and navigating from A to B in this sprawling city. Training has been challenging and, at times, lonely. To counter that, I joined the London City Runners, who meet on Tuesday evenings near my work to run along the Thames. They also have a Wednesday track session, which has been great for getting my legs moving, meeting new people, and providing extra motivation.

In between, I've managed to fit in one to two strength sessions a week. My weekly mileage could have been better, but I've focused on staying healthy, strong, and consistent. Given the emotional toll of all the changes, I believe this approach is more important than pushing my body to its limits. This journey isn't just about running a race; it's about embracing every step, every challenge, and every bit of the process. It's about proving that we can achieve incredible things with heart, determination, and the support of those around us.

Being away from my family, dog Storm, and friends has been more complicated than I anticipated. I haven't even moved into my own home yet. It's been a whirlwind of changes and adjustments. Things will settle and improve, I know that. I've been so fortunate with the people I've met here, but getting out the door has taken a lot of commitment to my training and discipline, especially when the loneliness creeps in. I've been making the most of the flexibility in my new role. On Wednesdays and Fridays, I have flexi-time as those are my Head of Rehab days. For example, the other day, I went to one of the clinics in the morning and decided to run during lunch. The weather was beautiful and the perfect opportunity to clear my head and explore more of London.

I made a point of focusing only a little on my pace or distance. Instead, I took it slow and enjoyed the sights around me. I snapped photos of things that intrigued me—odd-looking London buildings, endless murals on the walls, and a random arty statue in the middle of a walkway. It wasn't about the pace that day but about spending time on my feet and getting to know my new surroundings. It turned out to be a good day, with the run breaking up my work routine and giving me a bit of mental clarity. I finished off the day by catching up on some admin in the evening, feeling refreshed and ready to tackle the tasks.

But then there are the other days. The days when I have a session planned but feel so mentally and physically drained that even the thought of running seems too much. On those days, I've learned it's okay to go home instead. I focus on nourishing myself with a good meal full of fresh food and then try to get an early night. It's all about balance. In the remaining weeks leading up to the race, my biggest goal is to stay healthy and minimise stress. I want to keep my training consistent but also manageable. I need to prepare mentally for the race while ensuring I arrive at the start line as rested and prepared as possible. This journey is as much about listening to my body and needs as it is about pushing through the miles.

**Home**

Weekends are quiet for me in terms of socialising. I spend most of my time organising, going for a run, and planning the upcoming week—figuring out what time to leave the house, what food to buy (but not too much since I'll be leaving soon), and what to pack for the days so I can run from work and then head back the next day. But this particular weekend was different. It was a moving weekend, and I had much on my plate. The second cross-country league race was happening, and it would be my first one with the London City Runners. I also connected with a fellow South African who lived near the cross-country course in Wimbledon Common. On top of that, my sister was flying from Texas, USA, through Heathrow on her way to South Africa, and she had a layover for a few hours on Sunday. Naturally, I decided to combine all these plans with moving. It made sense at the time…

I was living in Woolwich Arsenal, east of Greenwich in southeast London. I packed up my life again, taking the tubes and trains across London to the west—Raynes Park/Wimbledon area. Since arriving in London, I hadn't bought much because I knew I'd be moving again and would have to navigate this kind of travel. My trusty app guided me on where and how best to get there. However, I didn't check for wheelchair access, so I ended up at two stations where I had to lug my heavy bag up the stairs. Someone offered to help at one point, but at another time, people just watched me struggle. I could have asked for help, but it's one of those things that goes both ways.

Eventually, I arrived at Bronwyn's place. Funny story—this was the first time we met in person! I had run with her husband, Grant, once in South Africa and had kept up with her on social media, but I had never met her before. We hit it off right away. They made me feel incredibly welcome and part of the family. We stayed up quite late on Friday night, chatting away, with plans to get up early for the Wimbledon Common ParkRun the following day. We got up and warmed up with a jog to the park run. This was one of the most extensive park runs I've seen in the UK, although I've only been to a smaller, newer one in the Woolwich area. The place was buzzing. It was a two-and-a-half-lap course. There were some announcements as we arrived, and we made our way to the start line. Off we went, running through the beautiful forest of the common. The ground was damp but primarily firm. We kept up a moderate pace, chatting away and enjoying the scenery. The marshals were incredibly friendly and supportive. As we finished, the crowd gathered and cheered us on as we had won, even though we came in around 180th place. It didn't matter at all. It was the perfect way to spend the morning.

After a quick walk back home to change, it was straight back to Wimbledon Common for my cross-country league race. I met up with the other ladies, and we went through our warm-up drills, getting ready for the start. It was a gorgeous day with blue skies and perfect weather, ideal for running. We were told the course was two laps of 3 km each, so I started near the back, which I quickly learned was a mistake. I got bottle-necked early on, and many runners slowed down on the downhill. I felt comfortable using technical and steep descents, so I slipped past them on the side.

At 3.5 km, I was deep in thought, trying to strategize how to pace myself for the remaining distance, when suddenly, I realized we were already on the second loop. My mind started racing—would there be a third loop to make up the distance? Should I push harder or hold back? Then, before I knew it, the finish line came into view. It turned out to be two laps of 2 km each, much shorter than expected! I was relieved but couldn't help feeling that I would have run the race a bit differently if I'd known. I learned that these runners aren't too fond of downhills, but I've come to embrace them, making it a key advantage for me.

After the race, I treated myself to a Greggs pie (a must in the UK) and some treats from Waitrose, then made my way back on the trains to Sevenoaks, Kent—my new home. Thankfully, there weren't many changes so I could relax on the 30-minute train ride. I caught a taxi from the station, as I wasn't keen on walking a mile with all my gear.

As I entered the house, I was overwhelmed with emotion. This wasn't just any house—it was our new home, where my family would soon join me, and we'd start our new life in the UK. It felt monumental. This was where we'd make new memories, explore the community, and participate in local schools and sports. Our fresh start, away from South Africa, had truly begun.

While all these thoughts ran through my head, the practical part of me quickly kicked in—I needed to figure out what essentials I needed to live here for the next few weeks before heading back to South Africa. The house was unfurnished, with only curtains, a fridge, stove, bin, and washing machine waiting for me. It was already 6 pm on a Saturday, so I set off into the night to find the nearest shop. I bought only the essentials—food, washing-up liquid, a spoon, a kettle, and a mug—knowing I'd have to carry it all back home on a 35-minute uphill walk. I was utterly spent by the time I got home, but this was home now. It was my space and felt like the beginning of something new and hopeful.

I had two weeks in this house before returning to South Africa for my 100-miler and to see my family and friends again. One evening, while walking home from work, I encountered a food vendor on my road. Living on a cul-de-sac, I found this entirely unexpected, but it was a delightful surprise. Two lovely ladies were selling Greek street food, and they were there regularly, they told me. I decided to try their weekly special, and it was delicious—an unexpected little joy.

Settling in has been an ongoing process, and it's not just the physical activities that take a toll. My mind has been working overtime learning new things, from navigating my surroundings, adjusting to UK systems, and figuring out the house itself. The heating, for instance, was a challenge. I spent two days trying to figure out why it wasn't working. I had the timer on, and the switch on the wall was lit up, but no heat. Finally, I realised there was a second timer downstairs that needed adjusting. Once I turned it up, the house warmed up, and I could finally relax. It was a small victory, but a victory nonetheless. Thankfully, the weather wasn't too cold, and being in a terraced house meant the place stayed relatively warm.

These little accomplishments remind me that I'm slowly building a home and a life here. Bit by bit, it's all coming together.

As I approach the final week leading up to my 100-miler, I've reflected on how much the journey has shifted from my original plans. I had envisioned immense training sessions packed with mileage, elevation, and night runs. I had intended to fine-tune my gear during long outings, ensuring everything was dialled in perfectly. But life had other ideas, and instead, I found myself moving countries, trading hills for the flat terrain of London, balancing the chaos of moving, starting a new job, and just maintaining the basics like eating well and keeping up with laundry.

But you know what? It's ok. I've learned that adaptability is one of the most critical skills in life, not just in ultra-running. This 100-miler will likely unfold differently than I envision. There will be moments that exceed my expectations, but also, without a doubt, some callous times. And the unexpected is always lurking around the corner. The mental game, though—that's where I've been sharpening my edge. Ultra-running is about more than physical endurance; it's a mental battleground—this part of the preparation I've covered in abundance. With all the change, adaptation, and challenges over the past few months, my mental resilience is more vital than ever. I've kept running, even when I didn't feel like it, and I've kept my eyes on the prize—staying healthy and strong for race day.

## One Week to Race Day

With just a week to go, I'm feeling the weight of everything. I've moved into a new home, work is busier than ever, and I'm loving it, but it's taking a lot of my energy and focus. My commute was longer, and I slept on the floor for three nights with just a sleeping bag and cushion. I've upgraded to a blow-up mattress, and while it's better, it's not ideal, leaving me stiff in the mornings. My "sofa" is a blow-up chair in the living room—not exactly what you'd call luxurious comfort when I'm trying to relax after a long day. I miss my family, my friends, and the familiarity of home. I know this phase is temporary, but it doesn't make it any less challenging right now. My body, mind, and emotions are tired, which isn't surprising when I think about everything I've been juggling. The emotional strain of this move, planning for the race, and adjusting to a new life has taken its toll.

Thankfully, this weekend is quiet, and I can finally focus on rest and recovery. I don't know how the race will unfold, but I will give it everything. I've done my best to plan, study the routes, get advice on unfamiliar sections, and ensure my kit, gear, and fuelling strategy are ready. I've kept in close contact with my support crew, reviewing what I'll need and expect from them on race day.

I realised recently that I hadn't checked the compulsory kit list for a while, so I returned to the UTCT website. Of course, they had updated it, and I still needed waterproof trousers (or "pants" as I keep calling them, forgetting I'm now in the UK) and a beanie. Luckily, I ordered those last-minute items and received them just in time to finish packing.

I love this part of the process—the planning, the prep, the lists, and mapping out potential race scenarios. I've worked out timings for different finish possibilities and made detailed notes on what to expect during the race, factoring in the ever-unpredictable Cape Town weather. Currently, the forecast looks favourable, which is rare for Cape Town, which is known for serving four seasons daily. The race will take us through terrain that climbs and descends continuously, meaning I could be battling rain and wind on the mountain tops and sweltering heat as I descend. It looks like moderate weather, but I'm preparing for all the possibilities.

I've set myself two critical goals for race day:

1. **Finish.** I will start slowly, walk the hills, use my poles, and take in the views and the support around me.

2. **Live in the moment.** I've spent a year dreaming about this, training for this, and sacrificing for this. Now, I want to make the most of every step, every challenge, and every triumph.

I'm ready. Let's see where this journey takes me.

As the days count down, I keep reminding myself to smile and enjoy. This is my choice—an adventure I've chosen to explore, to embrace, and to make the most of. The inaugural 100-miler for Ultra Trail Cape Town (UTCT) is a challenge I've been preparing for, a dream that has consumed my thoughts and training for the past year. Last night, I dreamt that I finished the race. It was hard, long, and painful, but I kept moving forward, and eventually, the finish line came into sight. I crossed it, crying with joy. Maybe that's how it will be, or it will be pouring rain, making every step feel like a battle. But no matter what happens, I've envisioned myself finishing, and I genuinely believe I will.

This race is massive—166 kilometres with over 7,000 metres of elevation gain. We have 45 hours to complete it, starting at 5 PM on Friday, 25th November, and finishing by 2 PM on Sunday, 27th November. Two nights out on the trail, pushing beyond limits I didn't know I had. This will be the hardest, longest, and most gruelling event I've ever done, but it's not just my race—it's a team effort. I couldn't even get to the start line without the incredible support from my family, friends, and all those who have helped me prepare.

There's an African saying that I've always loved: "It takes a village to raise a child." It reminds me that running an ultra is the same. It takes a whole community to support someone through something as monumental as this.

With just six days to go, the planning is in full swing. I've set up a WhatsApp group for my supporters so they can track me along the way, and my followers will share my progress through a tracking app, sending live updates to family and friends. I won't be checking the group during the race, but knowing they're all cheering for me strengthens me. It got me through the 13 Peaks Challenge and will help me push through this 100-miler, too.

I'll be on a plane to Cape Town for four more hours of sleep. I've been testing how to pack all my essential gear into my hydration vest, trying different setups to ensure everything fits and feels right. It's crucial to get this sorted before the race. I'm also packing "normal" clothes for my time in Cape Town—a strange thought since all my focus has been on race gear! I hope I can sleep on the flight, though I usually watch movies instead. But I'll do my best to rest and conserve energy this time.

One of the best birthday presents I bought for myself this year has been my Bluetooth Shokz. I've used them daily, commuting to work and during my 50 km race. They're fantastic because they don't sit inside your ears—they use bone conduction, which means I can still hear my surroundings while listening to music. They'll be a great companion during the night sections of the race, especially when the fatigue sets in. I've been building a playlist called "Inspiration," I know it will carry me through those dark hours when I'm tired and the second night on the trail feels endless.

The first night, I'm confident I'll be able to handle it—I know the terrain well, and I'll still be relatively fresh. The second night will be more challenging because of the exhaustion and the unfamiliar sections of the route. But that's when my playlist, some caffeine, and my relentless "step, step, step" mindset will kick in. I'm ready to embrace every moment of this challenge.

**Friday, 25th November 2022: Inaugural Ultra Trail Cape Town 100 miler (Cape Town)**

The journey to the airport on Wednesday, 23rd November, went smoothly. I arrived at London Heathrow packed, ready, and full of excitement. The self-service check-in area was surprisingly organised, with just a few people assisting, as most of it was done electronically. I was flying to Cape Town via Munich, and despite a smooth flight, I could not sleep. Not even a wink! Frustrating, I used the time to watch movies, close my eyes, and try to stay hydrated. The hours passed quickly, and soon enough, I was greeted by the stunning backdrop of Cape Town's mountains and the familiar warmth of South African accents all around me. Leon, a friend and fellow UTCT 100-miler, picked me up from the airport. We went to my parents' home in Claremont for a quick hello and immediate unpacking.

Though it was still early morning, I knew I had precious little time to organise everything for the race and my seconders before registering at the Gardens Rugby Club. One of my favourite parts of this entire adventure is the organising. I thrive on planning and preparation, especially when an incredible team is supporting me. Their belief in my dream brings it to life. My room quickly became a scene of organised chaos, with gear scattered across two beds. I meticulously sorted everything into piles—items for my seconders (extra clothes, gear, lights, fuel) and my race-day essentials. Lists were checked and rechecked, bags packed, and finally, I felt ready for registration. Despite my sleepless flight, I couldn't bring myself to rest. My body was buzzing with excitement, completely unaware of any fatigue. Looking back, I'm constantly amazed by how resilient and robust the human body is, especially after all the physical and emotional demands I've been through lately. I hadn't been sick. I felt strong. I'd been consistent with my training, and I knew from experience that, in ultra-running, the mind takes over after those first 30 kilometres.

Training the mind is just as important as training the body. It's a vital part of preparing for the unknown, the unexpected. You train the mind in many ways—

enduring challenging runs in adverse weather, solo night runs, and meticulously planning your gear and the route. One piece of advice I found incredibly useful was writing a race-day report *before* the event. I imagined how different points in the race would feel, when it would be daylight or dark, and how I'd react to other challenges. This mental rehearsal gave me a clear picture of what lay ahead and how I might overcome any obstacles.

Life is often a juggling act, balancing what's essential while staying focused on your goals. I sometimes get it right, but I try. I value the opinions of others and cherish time spent with loved ones because giving someone your time is the most valuable gift you can offer. I firmly believe in *carpe diem*—seizing the day with as much passion, joy, and energy as possible. Many people ask me how I manage to have so much energy. I've always felt it's a blessing, a gift from God. Enthusiasm and energy are contagious, and I love sharing that spark with others. If I can inspire and encourage someone and show them that they're capable of so much more than they believe, then my cup overflows. That's what drives me—showing people that they can dream big, work hard, and achieve goals that once seemed impossible.

And here I am, two days away from the start of a race that has been my dream and focus for so long. It's more than just a race—it's a culmination of training, faith, and the support of those around me. The countdown is on.

## UTCT 100 Miler Registration – Thursday, 24th November, 1 pm
Leon and I made our way to registration, quickly finding a parking spot on the steep, familiar roads of Cape Town. As we walked towards the Gardens Rugby Club, the reality of the race started sinking in. I couldn't believe I was back here, a year after signing up for the 65km, now about to tackle the inaugural 100 miler. The sun shone, and the sky was a perfect, clear blue, but the wind was howling. It kept the heat at bay, which was a blessing, though I knew the wind could be challenging later. I felt like a kid about to be handed the most significant ice cream ever—full of excitement and energy. I was practically bouncing as we entered the registration area, all smiles, buzzing with that pre-

race adrenaline. It was finally happening!

As I approached the 100-miler section of the tent, I couldn't help but think back on everything it took to get here. I moved to different countries, adjusting to life in flat, hill-less London and experiencing the many challenges that came with it. I had focused on what I could control—consistency, strength training, and staying as healthy as possible. Despite everything, I had made it to the start line injury-free, rested, and ready.

With multiple bags in tow—one for compulsory gear and two for my seconders filled with nutrition and extra kit—I was ready to get checked in. The lovely volunteer greeted me and informed me that I was the first woman to register for the 100 miler. That was a fun little nugget of information! It was reassuring to know that I was well-prepared as she meticulously went through my gear: headlamps, waterproof jacket, pants, chargers, and more. Finally, she handed me my race number—1110—and the iconic GPS tracker, along with a race shirt and 12 Maurten gels. The tracker, an added challenge to fit into my pack, needed to stay dry for the entire race. Another detail to figure out!

Once registered, we made our way to the expo, where I grabbed a few essentials from the Rock Rabbit crew—an extra bottle, my new hydration vest, and some lightweight gear to return to the UK. I then headed to the Salomon store to pick up a pre-ordered hoodie. This wasn't just any hoodie; it symbolised so much more. It was something to wear proudly after completing the race, a reminder of the challenges faced and overcome, and a celebration of this massive dream. When the race got tough, I knew I could focus on that hoodie and the sense of achievement it represented. The wind continued to howl as we wandered through the expo, taking photos with the fantastic Elixinol team, who had been so supportive throughout my training. Their encouragement, whether through gear, advice or just being there, had meant the world to me. Being part of a team like that was one of the reasons I love ultra running—it's not just about the individual; it's about the community, the shared purpose, and the deep, genuine care. I also ran this race for a cause close to my heart: Fit4Rhinos. Raising money for baby rhinos to provide their much-needed milk, which could amount to 18 litres daily, was part of my "why." The cause kept me going, and we managed to raise over R11,000 in the end.

I caught up with Denzil, who was registering for his 100km race, which started the following day. He'd tackled the 35km the previous year, and now here we were, both doubling (and more) our mileage. His calm presence balanced my boundless energy as we took photos with Leon. I also met with Liezl from FitGirl4Rhino for more pictures, dancing, and another cup of coffee—why not? We were soaking up the atmosphere, chatting with friends, and sharing that disbelief that we had made it this far. It was surreal, and the excitement was palpable. The countdown was on. With registration done and all the essentials in hand, it was real. I was ready for this adventure, knowing it would test every ounce of my physical and mental strength. But an incredible team surrounded me; we were all in this together.

Social media has always been a way for me to capture and share moments that matter, and registration day at UTCT was no exception. I couldn't resist grabbing Liezl and having her record me as my usual bubbly self, dancing around the registration area. As we spun around, I saw a few runners smile and heard the typical "Save your energy!" comments, but for me, this was my way of energising. Expressing myself, being alive, moving, and having fun— that's what fills me with energy. Dancing around in the moment's excitement is my way of celebrating being here, ready to take on this huge challenge.

It's funny now, looking back, how mild the weather seemed that day. The wind was gusty, but I didn't think much of it. It didn't feel like a sign of things to come. In my mind, once night fell, the wind would die down. But the weather had other plans for the weekend, and what we went through was far from what I expected. When I signed up for UTCT in May, I had everything meticulously planned—elevation training, mileage, support systems, and how to structure the months leading up to the race. But I never anticipated moving to London just eight weeks before, completely throwing a wrench in my plans. Suddenly,

I had no hills to train on, was away from family and friends, and was balancing the stress of adjusting to a new country, finding a home, and a new job. There were so many moments, especially when I was sitting on the train in London, where I thought, "What am I even doing? I must be crazy to attempt the 100 miler."

A few weeks before entries closed, an email offered the option to downgrade to a shorter distance—100 km. I thought about it. 100 km was still a huge challenge and would certainly be an achievement. I wasn't training on elevation the way I had planned, and it seemed like a reasonable choice with everything else going on. But then, another voice inside me was louder, more determined: *The 100 miler is the dream.* That's the challenge I had been preparing for and dreaming of for over a year.

Yes, things have changed, but isn't that what ultra-running is all about? Facing unexpected obstacles, adapting, and pushing forward despite everything going wrong? I realised that, in a way, all these changes were preparing me better for the race. Ultra running is never straightforward. The physical and mental challenges on race day don't care about your plans—they test your adaptability and grit. What I had been living through, the upheaval, the stress, the adjustments, was all training.

**I focused on what I could do and stopped looking at what I could not change.**

As I approached the UTCT 100-miler, I consciously decided to focus on what I could control and let go of what I couldn't. That was a significant turning point for me. The three pillars that I leaned on were:

- **Consistency** in training.
- **Strength work** to ensure my body was strong and resilient.
- **Mental training** is the often overlooked but crucial part of any ultra-run.

## Siblings

The night before the race was extra special because I got to spend it with my sister, Sue, who had come from America for the week. This was the only time we had together in Cape Town, as the race would take up my entire weekend, and she was due to fly back to Texas on Sunday evening.

I've always cherished my relationship with Sue despite the significant age gap. I am what Afrikaans speakers call a "laat lammetjie," meaning I'm the late lamb—the youngest, born long after my older siblings. My brother, Brett, is eight years older, and Sue is ten. Growing up, I often felt like an only child because by the time I was old enough to want to do things with them, they were already moving on with their lives, and I was still the little sister, often getting in the way, as younger siblings tend to do.

By the time I reached high school, Brett and I had developed a close bond, but Sue had already moved out, married at 19, and by 21, had relocated to Johannesburg while I remained in Cape Town. I longed to know her better, but the distance between us—physically and in life stages—made that problematic. Then, just before she and her family emigrated to America, Sue gave me the most beautiful gift: a plane ticket to Johannesburg to spend time with her before they left. I was 16 years old, and it was my first time flying alone. The thrill was indescribable, not just because I was travelling but because it meant I finally had the chance to spend quality time with Sue. She wasn't just my older sister anymore; she was becoming my friend, and the age gap didn't matter as much anymore.

Over the years, Sue has visited South Africa almost every year, and I treasure the time we spend together. I briefly lived with her when I took a gap year and au-paired in America. She's been a constant source of strength and support for me and having her with me in Cape Town the night before the biggest race of my life meant the world to me.

What made this trip even more remarkable was how it fell amidst so many life milestones for our family. Sue had already planned her visit but hadn't told anyone because Brett and I were navigating significant events. Brett had just won a trip to Malta to compete in the Settlers of Catan World Championship, becoming the reigning South African champion. I was preparing for my 100-miler while adjusting to life in London. Despite all of this, we managed to spend some time together. We even spent a day in London during her layover, exploring Windsor, tasting delicious doughnuts, and soaking in the joy of being with each other. Those moments, though brief, were priceless.

As the race loomed, having Sue by my side reminded me of the importance of family and the deeper connections that we sometimes take for granted. It also gave me the emotional fuel to face the challenge ahead.

I realised that when I finally arrived in Cape Town, I was catching the tail end of Sue's trip, and after the weekend, she would already be heading back to Texas. After my race registration, we managed to squeeze in one last evening together, and we decided to head down to the Waterfront. Looking back to our last time together, I fondly remembered how I had convinced (or instead strongly encouraged) my sister to get a sister tattoo with me. Sue wasn't keen on the idea of a tattoo at first. She was firmly against it. But then, one day, she got one on her own! After that, she didn't have much of an excuse in my eyes—if she had one, why not get a matching one with me? It became another special memory we shared, a permanent bond we could always look back on.

With Cape Town's vibrant energy surrounding us that evening, we made our way to the Waterfront. Sue had her eye on a unique ring she'd spotted earlier and wanted my opinion before deciding. The ring was stunning, crafted from elephant hair, with delicate gold elephants walking in a perfect circle around it. It was an intertwined symbol of beauty, strength, and nature, and I gave her my full approval. It felt like a meaningful piece, just like our time together.

Over the years, I've understood that family takes many forms. There are the people you're born into a family with—your blood relatives—and then there are the ones who choose you, and you choose them. Friendships, the people who stick with you through life's highs and lows, become just as much a part of your family. I value these connections deeply. Time is the one commodity we can never get back, so it's essential to use it wisely. Every moment we spend with the people we love is a gift, and I try to cherish each.

# Phase 5: Race Day

**Ultra-Trail Cape Town 100-Mile Race**
**(25 November 2022, 5:00pm)**

**Race Day Morning**

I woke up with a sigh, glancing at the clock. It was only 5:30 am. This was supposed to be the day I could sleep in, but my body had other plans. Restless thoughts and excitement had kept me tossing and turning all night. Even though the race wasn't starting until 5 pm, I already felt the buzz. My mind raced excitedly as I tried to quiet the butterflies flipping. I decided to lie in bed for a few more minutes before getting up to begin my day.

The breakfast routine was handled with calm efficiency. Then, I dashed back to my room to triple-check my gear for the hundredth time. My seconding bags were packed, my hydration pack weighed a solid 3.5kg, and everything felt ready—but of course, I couldn't stop myself from going over it all again. The morning raced by, and despite my efforts to keep my mind busy with messages to friends and sorting gear, lunchtime came way too soon. I hadn't done half of what I wanted to.

I jotted down a few thoughts, made some videos, and snapped a few photos to keep my focus. Thankfully, my sister arrived just in time, and I used her camera skills to capture a few memorable shots in my gear, moments I knew I'd treasure. I wrote two words on my hands—**Focus** and **Journey**—to remind myself to savour every second on the trails, enjoy the process, and keep my eyes fixed on the finish line. My friend Leon, also tackling the 100 miler, arrived shortly after lunch to pick me up. The moment I had arrived.

## Getting to the Start Line

It all became a blur after that. Time seemed to both stand still and fly by. All I wanted was to get to the start line and get moving. The race didn't begin until 5 pm, so I had hours to kill once we arrived. I took part in the **UCT Heart Study** for ultra runners to pass the time. It was fascinating—an ECG, cardiac ultrasound, and a full body composition scan before the race, with plans to repeat the tests after I finished. The study was designed to assess the impact of long-distance running on the heart's structure and function, and I was excited to contribute to research like this, knowing I'd learn a lot about my body in the process.

Leading up to this race, one of my concerns was that I needed to train more with a fully loaded pack. At 3.5kg, it was heavy. I'd done plenty of runs with my Rock Rabbit pack, but only with some of my gear packed in. However, all my strength training and previous trail running paid off. Once I strapped the pack on, it felt comfortable. It fits snugly, and as I moved around, I was relieved it didn't feel as heavy as I'd feared.

As the 55km runners began to finish their race, the energy at the venue was electric. The crowd cheered them in while the 100-miler participants huddled nervously nearby, rechecking gear, making last-minute toilet runs, and exchanging glances of excitement and nerves. Finally, it was time to step into the starting pen. As much as I wanted to start the race, a part of me felt that familiar pang of anxiety, wishing I could somehow be anywhere else. I knew I'd prepared well. I'd done everything I could, but nerves crept in. I didn't want to disappoint my fantastic team of seconders and friends who had invested so much time and energy into supporting me for this monumental day. Their belief in me kept me grounded. I was grateful for their presence, especially for those friends who calmed my nerves before I stepped into the start pen.

The pen was empty when I entered, and I purposely positioned myself to the side, near the front, but not right at the line. Trail runners have a different vibe from road runners—many tend to hold back and only move forward when the race is about to begin, unlike road runners who fight for that front position. I took a deep breath.

Said a prayer.

And laughed out loud.

It was time.

## Gardens Rugby Club to Signal Hill

The nervous energy was palpable as I stood at the starting line with 154 other runners. Among us, only 11 women had entered this inaugural 100-miler. The atmosphere was electric, a mix of excitement and nerves, and the countdown suddenly began. It was time. We were off.

Despite the adrenaline urging me to shoot out with the pack, I consciously pulled back, reminding myself of my plan. This was a long weekend, not a sprint. I needed energy conservation, so I took it easy, especially at the start. But a small wave of panic hit me almost immediately—my map wasn't on my watch. I had started my timer but still needed the GPX map for navigation. Fiddling with my Garmin Fenix, I remembered holding the middle button would bring up more options. Sure enough, I found the course and selected "UTCT 100." A silent sigh of relief.

The wind already whipped around us as we looped around the rugby grounds, pushing us forward onto the steep downhill streets. I consciously checked my pace, knowing it would be easy to start too fast. Then, the first climb appeared within the first 3 kilometres. I was relieved to see others walking the steep incline, so I joined them, switching into my fast hiking mode. When the terrain levelled off, I settled into a steady run.

As we moved up the side of Signal Hill, the rhythm of bodies became synchronised, and there was a quiet unity as we tackled the trails. The air was cool, but the wind was already making its presence known, whipping across the path and pushing us off balance at times. Emerging onto the top road, we began the winding route towards Signal Hill's first aid station. I checked in quickly and continued, rounding the base of Lion's Head, the iconic silhouette looming as the wind howled in the background.

From there, we were headed towards the Kloof Nek aid station, where the first familiar face appeared. As I approached, I heard a loud, encouraging holler from Sam, who was marshalling. We had only connected on social media before, but her recognition and excitement lifted my spirits, bringing a huge smile. It was a small moment, but hearing that encouragement meant the world to me as I powered through towards the next stage of the race. The journey was beginning, and I felt ready for whatever lay ahead.

## Kloof Corner to Platteklip Gorge

As I arrived at Kloof Nek, the second aid station, I was greeted by Grant, with Liezl right beside him, offering me nutrition and her incredible encouragement. She was one of my seconders, always there with her infectious smile, ready to support me in any way possible. I didn't linger long, grabbing some potatoes as I walked through the station. My rule was simple: I'd always take nutrition from my seconders, no matter how I felt. With nightfall quickly approaching, I started the ascent up Kloof Corner. The atmosphere shifted as darkness descended, but the energy from the supporters still climbing down the famous Kloof Corner lifted my spirits. Some were wielding cowbells, beers in hand, cheering us on with wild enthusiasm. Their voices echoed through the night, boosting backmarkers like me, who still had a steep climb ahead. Their energy pushed me up the final, gruelling section before I reached the contour path leading to the infamous Platteklip Gorge.

As the sun finally set, the temperature dropped, and the wind increased in intensity. It was a clear but harsh night, with the wind howling around us relentlessly. Headlights were switched on, and though the sunset had been stunning, the wind overshadowed any comfort it might have brought. Approaching Platteklip Gorge, a section I had climbed several times before, it seemed longer than ever. The solitude crept in, and for the first time, I felt how lonely the climb could be. Near the summit, the biting wind made it impossible to keep going without putting on my rain jacket. I struggled to get it on as the wind tried to tear it from my grip. I had to carefully place my poles down, using both hands to secure the jacket as I leaned against the rocks to avoid being pushed over. It was a battle to keep my footing.

Finally, as I reached the last climb, I caught sight of the volunteers at the top. They looked like angels, standing in the cold, battling the wind along with us. One woman was huddled in a sleeping bag, nestled in a crevasse with her beanie pulled down low, while the other volunteer, bundled in numerous layers, was standing to tag and time us as we sumitted. Their dedication was remarkable. I thanked them as best I could, although I don't think I fully grasped the lengths they had gone to be out there for us at that moment. Their presence made all the difference, and I carried that gratitude with me as I continued.

## Table Mountain – Scouts to Llandudno

It was pitch dark as I ascended the top of Table Mountain, with two runners ahead of me. I tried to match their pace at first, but they were moving too quickly, and I soon decided it was wiser to settle into my rhythm. The flag markers were well-placed, shining brightly in the lamplight, guiding me through the darkness. Tall flags fluttering in the strong Cape wind, with green, yellow, and red reflective tape solidly pegged into the ground, stood like sentinels marking the trail.

The wind was relentless, and my poles kept knocking into my legs, causing me to stumble. It was better to pack them away and rely on my balance as I navigated the uneven terrain. Alone in the silence of the night, I felt strangely comfortable. The map on my watch worked fine, and the markers were clear, keeping me on course. I tried to play some music, but in the absence of a signal, my app failed to load, so I resigned myself to the sounds of the wind, my breathing, and the rhythmic bounce of my footsteps.

I passed a couple of runners along the way who were replacing their headlamp batteries, and I'm grateful that mine were still going strong. Another runner passed me with a quick greeting, their headlamp bobbing into the distance. I reminded myself to stick to my plan, run at my own pace, and stay cautious on the technical sections of Table Mountain. This was no time to risk injury.

My thoughts wandered back to all the training runs leading up to this moment, especially the nights spent running in the dark. It felt surreal to think I was finally living the dream, running the 100-miler I had been working toward for over a year. Soon, I spotted the Scouts' aid station lights at the top of the mountain. It was past midnight by now, and though the air was cold and the wind fierce, the volunteers were warm and full of energy, eager to help us in any way they could. After refuelling and using a proper toilet, I pressed on toward the steep descent into Llandudno.

This course section was familiar, though I had never done it at night. The wind howled, and the darkness made everything feel more treacherous. The steep descent involved using metal grips set into the rock and, at one point, a short rope to assist in descending a particularly slick rock face. I encountered a fellow runner who was struggling with the grips. I stayed with them, offering advice on where to place their hands and feet until they felt confident enough to continue. As I descended the contour path toward Llandudno, my anticipation grew. I knew my seconders—Se7en, the hoods, Liezl, and her husband Wynand—would be waiting for me at the next aid station. A huge grin spread across my face when I saw one of the hoods outlined by the road lights. This was more than just an aid station; it was a reunion with friends who had supported me.

The atmosphere at the Llandudno Lifesaving Club aid station was warm and welcoming. My seconders had set up a table with food, and they immediately sat me down with a hot cup of coffee in hand. This would become a cherished ritual throughout the race—coffee, food, and the sound of "Victorious" being played every time I arrived or left an aid station.

I was surprised to see Leon sitting at the table. I had expected him to be far ahead of me, but he had twisted his ankle and had been sitting there for half an hour, trying to refuel and decide whether to continue. My energy was renewed, though, and after a much-needed visit to the toilet (which took longer than expected, thanks to my pants sticking to my weary legs), I felt ready to head back out.

I spent around 15 to 20 minutes refuelling and ensuring I had restocked my supplies. Leon was still uncertain whether to continue, but I had rested enough time and was eager to press on. It was now around 1 AM, and while the world around us was quiet, the wind continued its relentless howl as I made my way out of the aid station, ready to tackle the next stretch of the race.

## Llandudno – Rocket Road - Hout Bay

Leaving Llandudno just before 2 a.m., I felt surprisingly refreshed. The excitement of the race still fuelled me, and even though it was deep into the night, there was a sense of peace in the solitude. Headlamps dotted the trail ahead of me, some runners passing by, others keeping pace, their bobbing lights creating a rhythm of movement in the dark. The trail was runnable at first, gently rolling, then transitioned into rocky coastal terrain with boulders to climb across as I made my way along Sandy Bay. Despite the challenging sections, it was invigorating, especially under the starry sky.

After the sandy beach, I knew the next big challenge was coming: Suther Peak, or as some of us called it, "Suffer Peak." I'd done this climb before during my 13 Peaks challenge, so I was mentally prepared for the 2 km grind ahead. Out came the poles, giving me extra support as I tackled the ascent. Nearing the top, the trail turned from a path to a scramble, with boulders and rocks that required both hands to navigate. The wind howled around me, but I finally reached the summit. The descent from Suther Peak was a new section for me, and I welcomed the opportunity to discover a different side of the mountain. It was a beautiful downhill, winding gently on a runnable path that allowed me to pick up some speed. The stillness of the night and the rhythmic crunch of my shoes on the dirt kept me focused as I made my way towards Rocket Road.

Rocket Road aid station caught me by surprise—it was just a tiny table set up on a dusty road, with two volunteers operating it. I quickly restocked, grateful for their presence in the middle of nowhere, and set off again, knowing the next stop was Hout Bay.

I was 48 km into the race, and the early morning hours were creeping in. I found a renewed sense of energy with just 8 km to go until I saw Liezl again. The path had become less technical, and the promise of sunrise was starting to brighten the sky. As I reached Hout Bay beach, I stopped for a moment to take in the sight of the waves, snapping a quick photo. The beach was deserted, and though it was still dark, the rising sun hinted at the dawn of a new day.

But the journey across the beach wasn't without its challenges. A lagoon separated me from the next aid station, and there was no way around it without soaking my shoes. With a resigned sigh, I splashed through, my feet instantly drenched. But I knew Liezl had a fresh pair of shoes waiting for me at Hout Bay, so I trudged on, eager for a change.

As I approached Hout Bay, fatigue hit hard. I'd been awake for over 24 hours; the wind had worn me down, and my mind was starting to feel foggy. But just as I was feeling low, I was greeted by a surprise—Linda Doke, a legend in the ultra-running community, welcomed me with a big smile despite being on crutches. Her presence lifted my spirits, and we chatted as we walked towards the aid station. Her warmth and positivity were precisely what I needed.

Liezl and Wynand were waiting at the aid station, ready with everything I might need. I wasn't in the best shape mentally, and I'm sure I was a bit grumpy, but they were patient, offering me food and support. Liezl had gone above and beyond, preparing various snacks, including some incredible meatballs that hit the spot. I changed into dry shoes and socks, thankful for the chance to care for my feet before heading back out.

With coffee in hand and after restocking my supplies, I said my goodbyes and pressed on. I was 56 km into my 100-mile journey, with 2,800 metres of climbing in my legs and sleep deprivation creeping in. But despite the challenges, I knew I had to keep moving forward. There was no turning back now.

### Hout Bay –Silvermine - Kalk Bay aka hitting the wall
Climbing out of Hout Bay, my legs showed signs of fatigue. I felt a cramp in my calf, and when I tried to stretch it out, the front of my leg seized up. I winced, trying to walk it off while continuing the steep ascent towards Blackburn Ravine. Not long into the climb, two runners with 100-miler bibs came barreling past me, heading in the opposite direction. Confused, I asked if they were lost or everything was all right. Their brief response was a simple, "We're pulling out." The words echoed in my mind. Only 50 kilometres into the race, they had decided to quit. They weren't injured; they had chosen not to continue. I couldn't wrap my head around it. The race was gruelling, and we still had a long way to go, but that only strengthened my resolve. I knew this would be hard, but I had come too far even to entertain the idea of giving up. If I had to crawl, I would.

The following section was reportedly tricky to navigate, where the 100-kilometre and 100-miler runners intersected before splitting again. As if on cue, my GPX tracker struggled, making it hard to determine which path to take. I stumbled upon two other runners coming down a path they thought was correct but had turned out to be a dead end. We figured out the right way up together and soon saw the signage that split the courses. From there, they disappeared, and I was alone again. The switchbacks of Blackburn Ravine were endless. Each turn revealed another steep climb, and my legs were burning, my energy fading. The ascent towards Silvermine was challenging, and while I knew the timing mat awaited me at the top, I was disappointed there wasn't an aid station there to break the monotony. But in a way, it was better. Without a stop, I had no excuse to linger. Still, the thought of sitting on a rock for hours did cross my mind more than once.

The route past Silvermine was beautiful and brutal, the relentless wind whipping at my body as I tried to keep moving forward. All I could think about was reaching the next aid station, where I'd see my seconders again. The mental battle was raging—I was sleep-deprived, physically exhausted, and filled with doubt. How would I finish this race when I still had over half the distance and elevation? The winding jeep track after Silvermine felt never-ending, and the switchbacks before Kalk Bay seemed to stretch for miles. I was hitting the wall hard. I sent a voice note to Glen and Se7en, sobbing uncontrollably, venting about how I had only done 70 kilometres and couldn't fathom doubling that distance with even more elevation. I also messaged Steve, knowing he would understand as an experienced ultra-runner. His reply was calm and reassuring, but what stuck with me was Se7en's simple message: "Come to us. We have you."

When I finally arrived at the Kalk Bay aid station, I was a mess—emotionally drained, physically broken, and on the verge of quitting. But as soon as I was welcomed in, my seconders knew precisely what to say. Quitting wasn't even an option. Liezl had prepared a delicious burger, which I had been dreaming of for hours, and the most caffeinated cappuccino I could have asked for. Knowing I'd need it soon enough, they slathered me in sunscreen and refuelled my body and spirit.

Sophia, one of my seconders, knelt beside me, her voice firm but compassionate. "You signed up for this. You're doing it. You can finish." She had run ultras that made my 100-miler look like a warm-up, so I knew she wasn't exaggerating. When people like Sophia speak, you listen because they know what it takes. My brother, Brett, had been out looking for me on the trail but had missed me, only to rush back just in time to offer a hug and encouraging words from our supporters on WhatsApp. My sister, visibly unsure how to handle the situation, stood on the sidelines as Se7en took charge. I had asked if I could sleep for a bit, but they gently urged me to keep going until Blackhill, promising I could sleep there if needed.

I was torn between continuing and giving up. I wasn't in pain, just utterly exhausted and mentally shattered. The thought of being only halfway through the race and elevation was daunting beyond words. But Se7en's request was simple: "Give me ten more kilometres." I knew I could manage ten more kilometres. That's all I had to focus on—just the next small chunk of distance. I got up. And at that moment, I knew I would finish. The hardest part was over. My seconders had pulled me from the edge, restored my hope, and reminded me of the strength I had buried deep within. With renewed energy, I ran out of the station, feeling completely different from the one who had entered it.

From that moment on, quitting wasn't an option. I had my team, my faith, and my determination. Now, it was just about putting one foot in front of the other and moving forward, no matter how slow or painful the journey.

## Kalk Bay – Blackhill - Simonstown

Leaving the Kalk Bay aid station, my seconders' cheers still rang in my ears. Despite the exhaustion weighing on me, I felt renewed—invigorated by their energy and the simple but crucial reminder to focus on small, manageable goals. My next target was clear: Blackhill aid station, 10 kilometres away. Breaking the race into these smaller chunks would get me through, and although my mind was foggy, full of emotions and fatigue, I clung to this strategy like a lifeline. I ran for a short while along the coastal road, the distant cries of seagulls mixing with the smell of salt. Even though I was running on empty, the sea breeze brought a calming sense of perspective—an odd comfort amid the struggle. Soon, the steep uphill sections reappeared, and I transitioned back into a purposeful hike. As the road led onto trails, the terrain shifted again, now winding around Elsies Peak. The sweeping views of the bay below were stunning, but I focused on keeping my legs moving forward.

The paths here were well-maintained, narrow and bordered by bushes no taller than knee height. My pace was steady as I walked upward, weaving through Red Hill and enduring the soft, sandy paths that seemed to sap every ounce of remaining energy from my legs. Each step felt like a monumental effort, but I pressed on, fueled by the knowledge that the Blackhill aid station was drawing nearer. Finally, I spotted the peaks of the aid station tents. Relief washed over me as I walked the last few metres toward my team, my shoulders sagging in exhaustion. I'd made it. A massive sigh of relief escaped me as I was greeted by my incredible seconders, who had everything ready—a chair, a blanket, and what looked like a feast fit for a king. The tent was quiet, with just one other runner inside. I recognized the organiser of this particular station—an experienced ultra-runner and someone who had shown me many of these mountain paths in the past. But even though I admired his accomplishments, I could barely muster more than a quick hello before collapsing into the chair.

I pulled off my hydration pack, ate a mouthful of food, and immediately fell into a blissful 30-minute nap. It was, by far, the best sleep I'd had in days. When I was woken, I didn't linger. A trick I had learned was to get up quickly to avoid slipping back into a drowsy state, and it worked perfectly. As I stood up, I felt surprisingly refreshed, as though that short nap had revitalised me completely. While sleeping, my team refilled my hydration pack, ensuring everything I needed was restocked. Coffee was waiting for me, along with more food. I took in some calories, sipped on the coffee, and felt a surge of energy. There was no more doubt—I knew I had enough time, enough power, and enough willpower to finish this race. Renewed and recharged, I was ready to keep going, knowing that each step brought me closer to the finish line.

The aid stations throughout the race were a lifeline. Each was incredibly well-organised, with specific rules for seconding teams and an efficient crew to meet every need. At Blackhill, the setup was simple—just a table, a few scattered chairs inside a medium-sized tent—but it felt like an oasis. Sheltered from the relentless wind and sun, the tent provided a moment of peace and comfort amid an otherwise challenging journey.

The volunteers at this station, like many others, were ultra-runners themselves. They understood exactly what it took to get through an ultra and knew how to support the runners on the course. They asked the right questions—whether we needed help or preferred a space to regroup. Their quiet expertise and calm presence were exactly what I needed, allowing me to recharge without feeling rushed. Despite having had an extremely long day, having been set up since the early hours to welcome the front-runners, they were still warm and welcoming even for the backmarkers like me.

Before leaving, we had discussed the next crucial stage—Simonstown, which had a cut-off point. After some calculations, we figured I had enough time to reach it, even if I resorted to walking. This knowledge helped ease some of the pressure, though I knew the race was far from over. Outside, the wind was still relentless, blowing sand and debris into me with every gust. The temperature had risen, and it was now Saturday afternoon, with the sun glaring down. I was grateful for my sunglasses and cap, which protected me from the sun's intensity and shielded my eyes from the stinging sand.

One of the highlights of this aid station was my brother. He always knew how to get a laugh out of me, and that lightness was precisely what I needed. Humour was essential. It lifted me out of the depths of pain and exhaustion, breaking the spiral of negativity that could so easily set in during an ultra. After my nap and a hot cup of coffee, I felt gratitude. I was grateful for my incredible crew, who had supported me tirelessly and amazed at how well my body was holding up, pushing through the pain and fatigue. With renewed energy and a smile from my brother's humour still lingering, I set off for Simonstown, knowing that no matter how tough it got, I had the right team and mindset to see it through.

Leaving Blackhill aid station, I felt renewed. I hugged one of the hoods, took a deep breath, and set off with a bounce in my step, determined to keep pushing. The path ahead was firm, with soft sand stretching along its undulating terrain. Though I was walking, my pace was deliberate. The sandy sections, combined with the relentless wind, made it challenging to gain traction. Running didn't feel like the best option here—I was focused on saving my energy for the long haul, aiming to finish within the cutoff rather than pushing too hard early on. It was lonely along the trail, but I had my music to keep me company. I played the song lists I had carefully crafted with friends' favourite tunes, allowing myself to reflect on everything and nothing at all. My body had energy, but I knew I had to conserve it for what was still to come. As I passed the 86-kilometre mark, I focused on reaching the next milestone—Simon's Town at 96 kilometres, where the race would hit a pivotal point with 4,544 metres of elevation completed.

The descent into Simonstown brought a shift in scenery. I was on the road, thinking the aid station was approaching. In the distance, I spotted Grant, one of the hoods, speeding past in his car. He quickly realised it was me, parked, and joined me for the final stretch toward the aid station. He shared some uncompromising news—two other runners he supported had to withdraw from the race due to medical issues. That left me as the only one from our Durban group still running the 100 miler. We walked together, chatting along the road before turning up a steep path that seemed to stretch forever. I couldn't help but ask, "How much further?" more times than I care to admit. They kindly responded, "Less than what you've already done!"—the only answer that could keep me going.

Finally, we arrived at the Methodist church aid station. It was a warm, bustling hub of activity. As we entered, I noticed one of the other female runners just leaving, looking determined to get ahead. But my focus wasn't on competing with others; my goal was to finish, and I was racing the clock more than anyone else at this stage. Inside the aid station was a noisy, bustling scene with volunteers working tirelessly and runners milling about with their support teams. Se7en had already set up our little area with a hot cup of coffee ready for me. I was ushered to my spot and immediately took off my pack, feeling the relief of shedding its weight.

One of my first tasks was to empty my shoes, which had accumulated what felt like a cup full of sand from the last sandy section of the trail. I couldn't believe how much sand I had been carrying, but thankfully, my feet hadn't been too uncomfortable. I was grateful they hadn't been rubbing, as I would have needed to stop earlier. It was a better use of time and focus to press on toward the aid station rather than stop and fuss with my shoe mid-trail. After refuelling, rehydrating, and catching my breath, I knew the most challenging part was behind me, but the finish line was still a long way off.

### "Don't leave sand in your socks – metaphorically and literally!"

This became a mantra as I sat at the Simonstown aid station, reflecting on the metaphorical and literal grit I needed to push through the race. At the moment, I had no idea why people were staring at me strangely, giving me the occasional wide-eyed glance. It wasn't until my brother approached and asked, "Are you cold? You look like you're freezing." I was utterly confused. I didn't feel cold, so I asked, "Why?" He pointed out that my lips, mouth, and tongue were stained blue from the rehydration drink I'd been downing in large quantities. I looked like I was in the early stages of hypothermia! It was worth it, though—those electrolytes worked wonders. I tried my best to wipe the blue stain from my lips, but at that point, it was the least of my concerns. I had bigger things on my mind.

Sitting down with my team, I immediately began refuelling. The coffee in hand was comforting, but the surprise of a homemade pancake from one of the hoods was the highlight. It was simply mouth-watering and a treat that brought joy to my tired body. These small surprises kept everything fresh, breaking the monotony of the relentless run/hike through the trails. The ever-changing landscape was a constant reminder of why I was there in the first place. It was a privilege to be out in nature, a part of this race, and even when the trails got tough, I kept reminding myself of the reasons behind it all. I had chosen this challenge. I had sacrificed long hours, physical and mental training, and poured in resources to enter and prepare for this race. The words I had written on my hands—*Journey* and *Focus*—echoed in my mind, reinforcing my commitment to this dream.

The priority, as always, was getting off my feet and unloading my pack. That instant relief was something I looked forward to at every aid station. Then came the nutrition—I knew I needed to refuel quickly before the next section. But as I removed my shoes, I realised my feet were another story. I had been running with sand in my shoes for quite some time. The irritation was becoming noticeable. I decided to change into a fresh pair of socks, taping my feet with *Hypafix*—a thin, adhesive bandage I used to prevent further chafing on my heels and the pads of my feet. There was a deep sense of humility, knowing I was part of the inaugural race and only a handful of women had entered. That awareness pushed me further. I felt a responsibility—not just to finish but to show what I was made of. Some people's doubts before I started the race were counterbalanced by an overwhelming wave of support from my friends. Their belief in me became another energy source I drew upon in those moments of doubt.

With fresh socks, patched-up feet, and a renewed sense of determination, I felt ready to tackle the next section of the race. There was still a long way to go, but the only way forward was one step at a time.

Navigating the aid stations during an ultra-marathon always came with its unique challenges, but none more so than the dreaded "toilet stop." I seized the opportunity if I even remotely thought I might need to go. The difficulty wasn't just finding the restroom; it was dealing with the sticky, sweat-drenched tights that seemed to have a mind of their own. Getting them down felt like an obstacle in itself. Picture me doing what I can only describe as a crazy limbo dance—stretching, bending, pulling—accompanied by a chorus of grunts and groans as the tights reluctantly peeled away from my legs. Every inch was a battle.

Once I managed to lower them enough to sit down, I had to be extra careful.

The moment my legs bent, they decided to remind me how many kilometres they'd been through, threatening to cramp with every movement. It was like an elaborate, carefully choreographed routine—hands on the walls, slow and steady, praying I could get through this without my legs locking up. It became a fine art, balancing relief with speed, knowing that the slower I went, the more likely my legs were to give out under me.

Then, oh, the relief… followed by the unexpected *burn*! That's when I realised I was probably under-hydrated, and the uncomfortable burning sensation while peeing served as my body's not-so-subtle reminder to drink even more liquids. We all know that unpleasant feeling. I made a mental note to gulp down even more water as I headed into the next section of the race.

But, just as I was basking in the relief of a successful toilet trip, the real challenge began—the dreaded reversal of the entire process. Yanking those tights back up was like summoning the strength of a thousand ultra-finishers. Now wrapped around my calves, it felt like they had fused to my skin. I groaned and grimaced, pulling and inching them up, one leg at a time, praying I wouldn't need to call in reinforcements for help. And if I did need to call a friend, how would I even explain that situation without collapsing into laughter or embarrassment?

After what felt like an eternity, I wriggled the tights back over my waist, ensuring everything fit properly to avoid the dreaded chafing. I was ready to carry on once I was satisfied with the fit, feeling like I had conquered yet another ultra-endurance challenge.

I couldn't help but chuckle at the idea of starting a blog post titled "Best Way to Go to the Toilet in Tights During an Ultra-Event: Top Tips." Honestly, it could become a best-seller!

Feeling a slight triumph after surviving the bathroom ordeal, I returned to the team—intact, a bit proud, and ready to gear up for the next leg. I mentally checked off each piece of trail gear as I gathered it, ensuring I had everything I needed for the next stretch. The aid station volunteers had already given my kit a quick inspection to ensure I was carrying all the compulsory gear, something that's strictly enforced in ultra races like this. Time penalties loomed over anyone found without the necessary equipment, but I appreciated the reason behind it. It wasn't just about ticking off a list. This gear could mean the difference between safety and severe risk in the remote, rugged terrain we were navigating, especially given the possibility of spending one or even two nights out in the wilderness, depending on your pace.

The debate about whether runners should be solely responsible for their safety or whether mandatory gear checks should be enforced has raged on for a while, but I firmly believe in both. There's a reason for having an essential gear list—it's about safety, not just for yourself but for the entire event. When you're isolated, tired, and deep into the night on a mountain, it's not the time to cut corners. With my race number securely pinned back to my chest—thanks to a mysteriously missing safety pin that was quickly replaced—I pulled on my hydration pack, reloaded it with snacks, and ensured everything was in place. I felt the familiar weight settle on my shoulders as I adjusted the straps, feeling ready to tackle the next section. Grant, ever the supporter, walked with me for a few steps, recording a short video farewell for the WhatsApp group. The group had been cheering me on from afar, and I knew that these little updates kept them connected to my journey.

With a wave to the camera and a quick jog for effect, I turned and set off once again, heading towards the next challenge—*the endless stairs*.

### Kleinplaas Dam – Kommetjie - Noordhoek

I left Simonstown with the warmth of the aid station still lingering, only to be quickly greeted by the steep roads leading me back onto the trails. The wind, a constant companion since the start, continued to howl as I climbed, but my mind was preoccupied with Se7en's brief description of the following section: *The Signal School Steps*. It is a classic stone staircase that never ends. And she wasn't kidding. I counted the steps as a distraction, but that didn't last long. Next, I tried counting the sets of stairs, but I lost track again. I eventually gave in to the fact that I'd have to keep stepping until I *saw* the top rather than hoping for it. Step after step, I moved upwards, my music playing softly in the background, pushing me forward as I climbed.

At last, the endless steps ended, and I was rewarded with a breathtaking view from the top. The sea stretched out before me, shimmering in the late afternoon sun. The salty scent of the ocean filled the air, and the caw of seabirds echoed above the constant wind. It was a moment of peaceful solitude, a reminder of why I loved being out in these wild spaces. The path flattened out, and I shifted into a steady pace, following the trail markers that had become my companions. The next stretch was gentle, winding toward Red Hill and onto the Hoerikwaggo trail, with jeep roads and flowing single tracks that were easy on the feet. It was late afternoon, and the sun shone brightly, though the wind continued to whip across the landscape, making it difficult to maintain any regular running pace.

I was mostly alone, as I had been for much of the race. But I was comfortable with that. Switching between my music and nature's sounds, I kept my body moving steadily forward. Physically, I felt good. My legs were holding up, and I had settled into a rhythm of fast hiking, occasionally breaking into a jog when the wind wasn't battering me too much.

Despite the conditions, I was determined to conserve my energy for the remaining miles. The trails wound through more jeep tracks and brush, leading me towards a small water point. As I approached, I saw a car parked with just a few bottles of water laid out for refilling. A person was sleeping in the front seat, and no one seemed to be around. It starkly contrasted the enthusiasm and support I'd encountered at previous aid stations. It wasn't what I had expected, and I felt disappointed for the first time on the trail. I refilled my water quickly, shook off the feeling, and kept moving. I reminded myself that the real goal was still ahead—*the finish line*—and I wasn't about to let one quiet moment dampen the momentum I'd built.

I took in the rugged surroundings as I topped up my bottles and slowly walked around Kleinplaas Dam. The dam was flanked by low brush and the ever-present jeep track stretching out into the distance. I had just hit the 100km mark. In that quiet moment, I allowed myself a small, personal celebration. I had almost gone further than ever in any race before, and surprisingly, I still felt good. But that victory was short-lived as my bladder decided to make itself known, and I realised I desperately needed to wee. I hadn't seen another runner since leaving the last aid station, and, of course, the longer I waited, the more I felt confident I'd see one the moment I stopped. Eventually, it became too urgent to ignore, and I darted off the path, taking the fork that wasn't part of our route. Hurriedly, I wrestled with my tights and squatted down. The timing, as always, was impeccable. My bladder seemed determined to take its sweet time, and my legs began to cramp as I crouched there, silently urging the process to hurry up.

After what felt like an eternity, relief finally came. I yanked my tights back into place and returned to the trail, laughing to myself. Not a minute later, a runner rounded the corner! I breathed a silent sigh of relief, though deep down, I realised that I didn't care much by now. In moments like these, necessity takes over, and you reach a point in ultra-running where modesty fades away. The priority is simply doing what you must do, and most fellow runners understand that. The southern section of the race was unfamiliar territory for me. I had researched the elevation and asked for tips, but there was a sense of venturing into the unknown. The terrain was runnable, but the constant battering from the wind made it challenging. I kept reminding myself to conserve energy. I knew I had another night and morning ahead of me, and pacing was crucial if I wanted to finish strong.

The landscape stretched out with endless paths, bordered by scrubland. Occasionally, other runners would pass me, often in pairs, moving at a pace faster than I wanted to keep. I stuck to my plan, deciding to run my own race rather than burn out trying to keep up. After what felt like an eternity, the trail eventually led to a road, then back onto another path before finally descending towards Kommetjie Aid Station at the 112km mark. The final descent was technical, and I took it slow, though excitement was bubbling up inside me, knowing that my crew was waiting for me. I didn't want to risk a fall so late in the game. As I emerged onto the road, my heart lifted at seeing Se7en's family, brother, and the hoods all waiting for me with open arms.

Grinning from ear to ear, I picked up the pace, running downhill toward the aid station. The thoughts of Kalk Bay, when I had been ready to give up, felt distant. I was energised, my spirit lifted, and I knew deep down that I *would* finish this race. The road felt like a welcome reprieve after the uneven trails and its predictability was a relief for my tired legs. The Kommetjie Aid Station was buzzing as I arrived. Volunteers greeted me with ringing bells, cheers, and congratulations. The warmth and excitement of the moment were contagious, and I felt a renewed sense of purpose as I entered the moderate-sized tent that served as the aid station, ready to restock, refuel, and push on for the next leg of my journey.

My seconders sprang into action when I arrived at the aid station, guiding me to a bench they had reserved for me. Their main goal was to get food into me, but my immediate concern was getting my shoes off and shaking out the sand that had accumulated during the last section of the trail. I reached down to peel off my shoes and socks, feeling the sweet relief as my feet were finally freed from the grit. A juicy chunk of watermelon was handed to me, and I greedily bit into it, not caring as the juice dribbled down my chin. It was refreshing, almost heavenly, after hours of relentless running. Meanwhile, the volunteers had prepared hot noodles, and I tried them. Each bite felt like a lifesaver, warm and wholly satisfying, revitalising my weary body.

As I settled into the usual refuelling routine, my mind turned to the discomfort I'd started feeling between my legs. Chafing. The dreaded burn had set in, and I mentioned it to Se7en. She immediately offered me some Vaseline, but I waved her off, stubbornly refusing. This is where my fierce independence came into play, and I found it hard to accept help even when I needed it. However, I have been learning through this experience that it's crucial to have the right people in your corner who are willing to push you to make the decisions you're avoiding. I went to the toilet and quickly realised how uncomfortable the chafing had become. Trying to wee while making strange grunting noises between breaths, I knew I had no choice but to swallow my pride. After a tug-of-war with my tights and some more discomfort, I sheepishly returned to Se7en, admitting defeat and asking for the Vaseline.

Heading back to the portable loo, I applied the soothing ointment, feeling instant relief. I was grateful for the nudge from my crew and realised that addressing the minor issues immediately could prevent them from snowballing into something far worse. Once sorted, I felt lighter, more comfortable, and ready to move forward again. The walk back to the tent, however, was its battle. The wind, still relentless, tried to knock me sideways with every step. I hoped that the gusts would ease up as the sun began to set, but I had a growing sense that the wind wasn't going anywhere. From start to finish, this race seemed to be defined by the wind's constant push and pull.

The tent at the Kommetjie aid station was alive with the buzz of other runners and staff, but I found my little sanctuary in the corner where my seconders took care of me. Brett, sitting next to me, was a lifesaver. We laughed hysterically, making silly watermelon smiles for a picture, and it was such a stark contrast to the darker moments I'd experienced back in Kalk Bay. It's funny how, in ultra races, you can swing from the lowest of lows to the highest of highs in hours. This was a lesson I kept reminding myself that no emotion, good or bad, lasts forever.

The burger handed to me was exactly what I needed. I devoured it, savouring every bite, and the noodles that followed were surprisingly delicious and filling. I always find variety vital during these long races—mainly whole, savoury foods. They're what keep me going.

I took off my shoes and socks, laughing as a small pile of sand poured out, adjusted everything, and felt like a new person. Those small changes—taking time to sit, eat, laugh, change shoes—made a world of difference, giving me the fresh energy I needed to tackle the next section of the race. While I was being tended to, the rest of my crew sorted out my hydration and fuel for the next leg. They were always one step ahead, ensuring I had what I needed until I would meet them again in the early hours at Noordhoek.

I couldn't help but be impressed with the course markers. Despite the brutal wind, most were still standing strong, guiding us along the way, which was essential given the unpredictable weather. When it was time to leave Kommetjie, I said my goodbyes to my incredible crew and started walking towards the beach. But almost immediately, I hit a confusing moment—I felt like such a fool! I checked my watch, then looked around, trying to figure out where the trail went. It was just before sunset, and for a moment, I couldn't see any markers. I didn't want to backtrack to ask for help, so I aimlessly looked around until a couple of beach walkers, noticing my confusion, pointed me in the right direction. I followed their advice, spotting a marker by the fence, and walked across the rocks and onto the flat expanse of Noordhoek beach.

As the sun set, I stopped to take a few photos and recorded a video reflecting on the race so far. Thinking about how much my mindset had shifted in just a few hours was surreal. I was no longer doubting myself. I knew—without question—that I would finish this race. I had enough time, and I was stubbornly determined. The only challenge now was to keep moving forward. The sand on Noordhoek Beach was firm by the water, but further out, it was soft and energy-sapping. Rather than running, I decided to walk fast. At this point, running would have drained too much energy, and I knew I still had a long night and many kilometres ahead. As the sun finally set and darkness enveloped the beach, I switched on my headlamp. It was just me, the roaring wind in my ears and the occasional headlamp bobbing in the distance from other runners. I could hardly hear the waves crashing beside me because the wind was so relentless, pushing me sideways with every step. Just before darkness took over, I spotted a little penguin playing along the shore—an unexpected moment of joy amidst the solitude.

Later, I discovered that Liezl and Wynand had been quietly following me along the road parallel to the beach, concerned for my safety. They didn't want me to know, but they were there, watching over me. It made me realise how incredible my support team was—they went above and beyond to ensure my race was as smooth as possible. All I had to focus on was running and moving forward. Everything else—the logistics, the planning, even the concern for my safety—was handled. It allowed me to switch off part of my brain that was no longer fully functional after so many hours on my feet and with little to no sleep. Their presence, even when unseen, was a constant source of strength.

As I trudged along Noordhoek Beach, I could feel the sand building up in my shoes. Each step shifted the grit under my feet, and though it was becoming increasingly uncomfortable, I convinced myself that it wasn't worth stopping to shake it out. I rationalised that every minute counted, and it seemed more important to push forward, especially since the next aid station was drawing closer—or so I hoped. Yet, in the back of my mind, I couldn't help but wonder if I was making a mistake. My feet were crucial to getting me to the finish line, and there was still a long way to go. This section of the race felt endless. The darkness had fully settled in, and though my headlamp lit the path ahead, the flags marking the course seemed to stretch farther apart with each passing minute. I thought I must be close to the aid station, but the zigzagging paths played tricks on my tired brain. Every turn revealed another stretch of trail, and the road seemed further away with each step. My mind, clouded by exhaustion and the strain of moving for nearly two days without natural sleep, was playing cruel tricks on me.

Finally, after an eternity, I climbed off the beach and onto a road. Relief washed over me as I spotted a few crew members waiting to guide me to the Noordhoek aid station. I kept asking them if we were almost there, my desperation for a break seeping through every word. The answer was always the same: "Almost there, just keep moving forward." And so I did, one foot in front of the other, even at a snail's pace.

When we finally arrived at the aid station, my sole focus was to get off my feet, empty the sand from my shoes, and refuel. A power nap would be heavenly if I could manage it. My crew could see the exhaustion in my eyes, but they were ready with food and encouragement, guiding me to sit down and take a breather. At this point, it was close to 2 am, and the weight of the second night without sleep was starting to press heavily on me. My headlamps had been a saving grace, illuminating the trail clearly, but my brain was no longer making decisions quickly. Simple tasks felt slow, as though my thoughts were moving through molasses. Yet, despite the mental fog, I knew one thing: I was still moving forward.

Delight and relief swept over me as I spotted the welcome banners at the Noordhoek aid station. The quiet atmosphere contrasted sharply with the internal turmoil; only two other runners were there—one exiting as I entered and another resting, refuelling. When I arrived, I heard murmurs about a fire, causing a potential reroute. Panic spiked within me at the thought that they might not let us finish the race. The fear of not completing this monumental challenge was crushing. But before my imagination could run wild, my crew quickly ushered me into the tent, sitting me down and shoving food into my hands.

Shoes off, pack refuelled, I allowed myself the luxury of a glorious 15-minute power nap on a camper bed. Flat on my back, it was as if I'd melted into the bed, my body grabbing whatever rest it could. But all too soon, I was gently woken with a cup of coffee, my crew nudging me back into action. Time was ticking, and lingering wasn't an option. I grabbed my pack, tightened my shoes, and, with my second wind, headed back out into the night.

The air was cool, but as it had been all race, the wind was the real enemy, slashing at me with relentless force. As I began the next section, I had only vague details about what lay ahead. I ran a short stretch along the roadside, my seconders driving slowly behind me, ensuring no vehicles would come too close. Then, the climb began.

For the first time in the race, I had company. Mike, another runner, joined me as we ascended the cliffside. His pole was broken, unable to collapse, making his climb even more precarious. The wind howled, determined to knock us off the narrow path, and I could feel it trying to push us sideways, making each step a battle. We pushed on, leaning into the climb, fighting the terrain and the wind together. Having someone next to me, even for this stretch, was a relief. We didn't talk much, but knowing I wasn't alone in this unforgiving section of the race gave me a slight boost of mental strength. Despite the wind and exhaustion, we kept moving step by step as the dark night held firm around us.

**Chappies peak to Hout Bay**
As I climbed Chappies Peak, I had to pack away my poles, using both hands and feet to scale the rocky face. It was pitch dark, but the race organisers had brilliantly marked the route, securing the flags deep into the rocks. The wind howled with unrelenting force, pushing me side to side, making it feel like I was fighting for every step. This section of the race was an absolute test of mental endurance. At one point, I made the mistake of looking up, and my headlamp illuminated the markers, stretching endlessly into the sky. It felt like I was climbing into the heavens, and for a fleeting moment, despondency washed over me.

But I quickly reminded myself how far I'd come. The thought of the sun rising in a few hours gave me a small beacon of hope—this brutal night wouldn't last forever. I wasn't alone either. Mike, the runner with the broken pole, was climbing ahead of me. We didn't talk much, as shouting over the wind seemed pointless, but knowing he was there was comforting. We silently encouraged each other to keep going, step after precarious step.

At times, the wind gusts were so strong that we had to cling to the rocks and wait for a brief lull before moving on. Later, I learned that the wind had reached 80 km/hour speeds—it certainly felt like it. Every gust felt like it could tear me off the cliff at any moment. After what felt like an eternity, the climb's summit appeared. My heart soared briefly, thinking we'd reached the top, only to realise it was a false summit. The climb continued.

Finally, the path began to level out, and the rocks beneath my feet felt more stable. We descended carefully, and Mike and I started to talk with the wind, now somewhat shielded. We refuelled and packed away the extra layers we didn't need anymore, and for the first time in hours, I felt a sense of rejuvenation. My legs had energy again, and the dread of the climb melted away as we chatted and moved at a good pace.

We spotted a lone volunteer on the mountain an hour later, directing us towards a detour. A fire had broken out ahead, making continuing on the planned route unsafe. We were to head down towards Hout Bay Road, where our seconders or taxis would transport us to the next safe section of the race at Constantia Glen. As we descended the steep terrain, the bobbing headlamps of the last 100-mile runners appeared behind us. They were close, but we were having a good time.

As we reached the road, my seconders were already waiting for me. But I urgently needed a wee before I could even think about heading off. Mike pushed ahead while I found a secluded bush, remembering to turn off my headlamp to avoid unwanted attention. Finally, relief! The detour shaved about 8 km off the course, affecting the 100-mile and 100-km racers. It was strange to think I had missed part of the planned route, but at that moment, I was just grateful to be safe and still in the race. My seconders whisked me away to Constantia Glen, ready for the next leg of the journey.

**Constantia Glen to Alphen Trail**
Mike and I huddled into the car, which sped off with urgency; our crew

determined not to let us waste a second. The car ride was filled with chatter, but there was a noticeable undercurrent of concern that I might hit a wall of exhaustion. Surprisingly, that wasn't the case. Instead of feeling drained, I was buzzing, realising I was on the brink of completing this monumental challenge. The reroute due to the fire hadn't unsettled me as much as I'd thought it might. I'd come to embrace it. In ultrarunning, as in life, you have to be adaptable. The quicker you accept the unexpected and adjust, the better off you are. That's a lesson I was learning repeatedly on this journey.

When the car finally pulled up at Constantia Glen on the Alphen Trail, it was still the early morning hours, pitch black and cold. With no time to linger, my crew practically shoved me out of the car, motivating me. Mike had already taken off ahead, eager to finish the final stretch. I started at a steady pace, savouring the moment. Alone in the dark, I was enveloped by the sound of the wind howling and the rhythmic pattern of my feet on the trail. The darkness was comforting, with the occasional reflective marker illuminated by my headlamp guiding me forward.

I felt at peace during this section. My legs were strong, my breathing relaxed, and I soaked in the tranquillity, listening to the sounds of nature slowly waking up. Now and then, I crossed roads and continued on winding paths that felt endless but enjoyable. I was approaching my penultimate aid station and started daydreaming about the food that awaited me there. The aid station, hosted by Sheena and Sian O'Keeffe, was known for its hospitality, and I knew I'd be treated like royalty upon arrival.

Sure enough, the lights of the aid station came into view, accompanied by the faint sound of music. As I approached, Sheena greeted me with a cowbell, cheering me on as if I had just won the race. The warmth of the welcome and the comfort of the aid station lifted my spirits even higher. My seconders were waiting for me inside the tent, ready with blankets and food. The temperature had dropped, so they wrapped me in a silver blanket while I surveyed the glorious spread of food. I could've eaten forever. The contrast between this quiet, serene aid station and the bustling atmosphere from last year's 65 km UTCT was striking. Last year, it was full of people buzzing with energy. It was just me, my crew, and the aid station team this time, but it was perfect.

I ate, laughed, and felt refreshed. I was ready to go. However, just as I left the aid station, my watch chimed. The battery was dying. I turned back to the worried faces in the tent, quickly explained, grabbed my Garmin charger, and set off again. I was determined that my watch would capture the entire journey. With 21 km left, I couldn't let it die now.

The darkness still enveloped me back on the trail, but I could feel the morning approaching. Shortly after leaving, I encountered a large log I needed to cross. Under normal circumstances, this would be easy, but in my sleep-deprived state, it felt like an obstacle course. Carefully, I placed each foot, focusing intently on not losing my balance. Once across, I breathed a sigh of relief and continued forward, knowing the finish line was growing ever closer.

## Nursery Ravine to University of Cape Town (UCT)

I find it hard to describe that feeling when you know that you are going to complete and absolutely nail a dream. I left the aid station with a spring in my step, knowing that I still had 21km of trail to cover before I stepped over that finish line, but knowing that I had more than enough time and the will to complete it. I wanted to savour every moment. I wanted time to stand still and enjoy it even more knowing that I was in the moment – never to be repeated at this time. It was realising that all the training, planning and sacrificing was worth it and especially when it came to my absolutely selfless friends who had taken their whole weekend and more to second me, push me and get me to the finish line. They believed in me, at times even more, than I did and they showed me that I could complete this 100 miler.

The birds were starting to wake up with their gentle calls. No one was around as I made my way up to Nursery Ravine and the well – known 400 steps. When someone says, "contour path", I used to have the misconception that it was a level path that you traversed along the side of a mountain with beautiful views. Alas, it can mean this, or it can mean climbing many stairs up and then down and then up again. There was around 800 metres of climbing to do from the nursery ravine aid station to the finish. Compared to what I had already done this was minimal, but it was still gruelling. I met up with one other runner as we made our way up to the nursery ravine section. In the middle of seemingly no – where we were checked at nursery ravine for our numbers. The next aid station was the final one at the University of Cape Town (UCT). I continued on as the path became a bit of a monotony. I was alone and suddenly desperate for the loo! I thought I could hold out until UCT but it just became too uncomfortable. At this stage it was light and the area that we were in was a very busy local trail area – not just for racers of UTCT! I took my chances and tried to go as much off path as I could and quickly – which did not happen due to fatigue and tights that at this stage were a second skin – squatted to wee. Problem number one – my legs were pretty smashed at this point and as I went into a glorious squat to relieve myself, I had to suddenly return upright as my muscles went into a semi – cramp! I was now even more desperate than ever and tried a second time more slowly.

Success! Then it seemed that this was going to be a Dawn record for longest wee ever. I was so desperate to end it as I knew at any point someone could come around the corner but another part of me could not care less. It was such an enormous relief to have emptied my bladder. As I scraped my tights up and put myself together once more, a runner came up from behind. I casually waved my greetings as though everything was absolutely normal. A close shave. In ultra running it comes to necessity and comfort and in the end not really caring at all what anyone else thinks. We are all in the same situation anyway. My legs were strong but at this stage my mind was starting to play tricks on me. I would have to consider each step that I took. I put my poles away as there are massively rocky, technical sections and I couldn't comprehend in my brain where to place both the poles (two of them!) and then my legs. So, I thought by taking the poles away I only had to think where to place my feet which was better. I seriously considered finding a rock space to lie down for 10 minutes as the fatigue was really setting in and I felt such brain fog. I was not imaging things or seeing weird objects like many people do, but I could not concentrate. I started to talk to myself and count my steps and just make sure that my footing was good so that I didn't sprain an ankle at this late stage. It was not worth it. I managed to step, step, step and make my way across. It seemed absolutely endless. The rocks, the undulating path and then finally headed downwards to, which I thought, was the aid station. I received an incredible surprise near the bottom section in the form of my long – time Cape Town running friend, Ruth and her husband James. They met up with me with some sustenance – toffees and bananas - and a huge encouraging smile. I felt really loved and needed the distraction with a friendly face and company.

I found that the race – although I enjoyed the solidarity at times – also became a little too lonely and I was grateful at the aid stations to meet up with loved ones and just having people around. We continued all the way down and I then asked if they knew where the UCT aid station was placed. They had changed it! Again, that mental aspect of expecting it around the corner but there was still a big climb before I reached it. I was so thankful to have Ruth walking with me and the encouragement was enormous as the blow to learning that the aid station had moved from the previous year could have got me down quite a bit. I made my way up the last little climb, saying my farewell to Ruth and James, and after what seemed like hours, I finally first heard then saw the crowd. Marlu was a lovely surprise as I neared the aid station and she had especially made her way down to see and encourage me. She has been instrumental in encouragement with my 13 peaks journey – running with us in the one section from Silvermine to Chapmans peak – and then in my UTCT 65 km she met me at the block house. I feel so blessed with amazing friends who take the time to support and encourage me in my goals and dreams.

It was bright sunshine with the pumping wind our ever – present companion. Huge hugs awaited me as I entered into my final aid station with my smiling crew. All I remember saying is I need to lie down for 10 minutes. Knowing I was so close to the finish yet had time to sleep was essential as I honestly was not thinking straight and I knew that a 10 – 15 min power nap would make all the difference and a lot more enjoyable final 10 km. It was also the nemesis Block house section which was an extremely steep climb up before traversing along the final path to Dead Mans tree, then down switchbacks to the finish line.

I crashed in the designated corner for sleeping runners. Before I blinked, I was being woken up and 15 minutes had disappeared. I was given a delicious cappuccino and the speckled chocolate eggs were a new and favoured snack at this stage. My stomach had started to feel a little unsettled so I did not take much in but knew I needed to eat something for the final 10 km of this incredible race.

## Homeward bound UCT to Finish via Dead man's tree

As I left the bustling UCT aid station, I couldn't help but feel an overwhelming mix of emotions. I was close to finishing, yet I wanted to savour these final moments. This was the culmination of not just months but years of dreaming, planning, and hard work. I had given everything to this race, and so had my incredible team of seconders who had supported me every step of the way. This was as much their victory as it was mine.

The final section started with the steep climb up to the Blockhouse, and I could feel the weight of every step as the wind continued to batter me. I kept expecting the 35km front runners to zoom past me, and when they finally did, I stepped off the trail to let them pass. Despite my exhaustion, I cheered them on, and in return, many congratulated me, realising I was one of the 100-mile runners nearing the end of my epic journey. The camaraderie was palpable, even as we all pushed our limits differently.

As I neared the Blockhouse, I felt a renewed sense of energy. The climb was tough but was the last major challenge before the final descent. When I reached Dead Man's Tree, I couldn't help but pause for a moment. This was it—the final stretch. From here, it was all downhill to the finish line. The winding descent was familiar to me from the 65 km race I had done before, and though the trail was rocky and technical in parts, I took my time to ensure I didn't trip or twist an ankle. I could see the rugby fields in the distance, and my excitement grew with every step. The closer I got, the louder the cheers became. People were gathered along the trail, clapping and shouting words of encouragement. It was almost lunchtime, and I could feel the crowd's energy as I approached the finish line.

In the last kilometre, I was thrilled to see my friend Mdu, who joined me for a short stretch, filming my final moments and congratulating me on my achievement. His support, along with so many others, had carried me through this monumental race. As I neared the finish line, I ran with everything I had left, grinning ear to ear, feeling the culmination of all my hard work and determination.

The moment I crossed the finish line was indescribable. My name was announced, my arms were raised in triumph, and my heart was grateful. I tried to cry, but the emotion was so overwhelming that the tears wouldn't come. Instead, I was embraced by my friends and seconders, who had been there with me through every high and low of the race. They knew how much this meant to me, and their pride and joy were evident in every hug and cheer.

I was handed the coveted 100-miler finisher's hoodie, which I was delighted to receive instead of the traditional buckle. I knew I would wear that hoodie with pride for years, a constant reminder of this incredible accomplishment. After crossing the finish line, I was whisked away to participate in the heart study I had signed up for. Lying down in the shade felt like a small slice of heaven after so many hours on my feet. I learned that they had to take down the tents at the finish due to the intense winds, which made me prouder that I had run through such brutal conditions.

I finished the race in just under 42 hours, having been awake for over 60 hours, save for a few power naps. Out of 155 starters, only 94 finished. I was the last of nine women to cross the finish line, and I couldn't have been prouder of that fact. I had pushed through every physical and mental barrier, and in the end, I had achieved my dream. This journey had tested me in ways I never imagined, but it had also shown me the depths of my resilience, determination, and the power of a supportive community. This was more than just a race—it was a testament to perseverance, to dream big, and to never give up, no matter how hard the road becomes. I will carry this experience with me for the rest of my life, knowing I can do far more than I ever thought possible.

# Phase 6: Post Race

### Reflections

The day after the race, I went through my phone, reading all the messages that had poured in over the weekend. My Wander Women were relentless in their encouragement, their voices resonating through the WhatsApp group like a constant cheer squad. Se7en, Liezl, and the rest of my seconders had been angels on this journey, guiding me, pushing me when I needed it most, and keeping me grounded. As I read through the endless words of support, I couldn't help but cry—first a few tears, then full-on sobbing. It wasn't sadness or exhaustion; it was overwhelming gratitude.

What took me by surprise was the sheer number of people who had been tracking my progress, cheering me on from afar. Friends, acquaintances, even those I hadn't spoken to in ages sent congratulations. It hit me then how much support I had unknowingly carried with me throughout the race. Each message, every word of encouragement, fuelled my determination, getting me through those challenging moments on the trail when I wasn't sure I could keep going.

I realised something profound in those post-race hours: the power of encouragement. You never know how a simple message or a few kind words can impact someone. It can be the thing that lifts them when they feel like giving up. I had felt this deeply during my race. It's a reminder that if you think of someone, send them a message. Reach out because you need to determine how much they might need it.

## So, what's next?

For now, I'm letting this experience soak in. I'm reflecting on how far I've come, not just in this race but in life. I've conquered something that, at times, felt impossible. I've pushed through mental and physical barriers I didn't even know I had. The next challenge will come; I know that because it's my nature to dream big and push myself. But for now, I want to take this time to rest, reflect, and express my gratitude for the incredible people in my life who have supported me on this journey.

I'll keep dreaming, keep running, and keep living with purpose. But right now, it's about soaking in the gratitude, the lessons learned, and the sheer joy of accomplishing something monumental.

Life consists of moments when we stumble, things fall apart, and failure feels overwhelming. But resilience is what makes all the difference. It's about rising again, learning from those setbacks, healing from the pain, and ultimately overcoming the obstacles that once seemed impossible.

Choosing resilience is choosing growth. It's embracing the challenges as opportunities to become stronger, wiser, and more determined. It's not the easiest path, but undoubtedly the most rewarding. Each time we rise, we prove to ourselves that we are capable of much more than we ever thought possible. Resilience isn't just about bouncing back; it's about bouncing forward. Living with resilience allows us to thrive, no matter what life throws our way. Embrace the falls because they make the rise so much more meaningful.

## Tattoos

Tattoos are such personal, meaningful forms of expression; for me, they've come to represent the different phases of my journey. I wanted to get one only if it genuinely meant something significant. Each one needed to be a visual reminder—a symbol of essential moments, milestones, or beliefs combined with the artwork's beauty.

My first tattoo came at a rough time in my life. I convinced my sister to get one with me, and after some resistance, she agreed. I needed a reminder of what mattered most—what was worth investing my energy into. We got a "family" tattoo shaped like an infinity sign intertwined with a heart. It was a simple but potent reminder of the people who were my foundation.

A year later, I felt like I was losing a sense of myself. I was trying so hard to meet the expectations of others and to keep the peace that I began to feel distant from the real me. I relented in too many ways and was compromising my values. That's when I decided on my "carpe diem" tattoo—a reminder to seize the day and stay true to myself, no matter the pressure to fit in or conform. It was my way of affirming what was important: making the most of every moment and living with intention.

When I faced another central turning point—leaving a stressful job and launching my physio practice—I marked it with another tattoo on my wrist. I chose the word "dream" with a butterfly. It was about embracing change and pursuing my dreams, even when I was terrified of failure. Starting my practice was daunting, but looking back, it was my best decision. When Covid hit, having the flexibility to work from home with my children was a true blessing.

Then, as if adding colour to my life, I enhanced my "carpe diem" tattoo with vibrant shades and added a small paper aeroplane on my shoulder. It represented flight, freedom, and the pursuit of dreams that carried me through each phase of life.

One of my most cherished moments came when my sister, who had previously resisted tattoos, finally got one with me. It was a matching "sister" tattoo. That ink on our arms symbolises our unbreakable bond despite our distance. It's not just a tattoo—it's a statement of our connection, blood, and love.

Another unique piece came to life during a women's group I attended. We were asked to paint anything that came to mind, and I painted a vision of myself standing on top of a mountain with a phoenix rising above me. That phoenix symbolises strength, hope, and the belief that no matter how tough life gets, there's always a way to rise above it. I later had this vision inked onto my shoulder, including a bit of addition—my border collie, Storm, standing by my side on that mountain. It's a reminder to keep looking up, to stay resilient, and to trust in God for strength.

2022 was a whirlwind year of change. I unexpectedly got offered a life-changing job in London, and within five weeks, I was living there, leaving behind my family and friends. I returned to South Africa briefly for my 100-mile race and to say goodbye correctly, and during that time, I celebrated my friend Nikki's 40th birthday most unforgettably. In jest, I had suggested getting tattoos together for her milestone birthday—and we did. We each got protea tattoos, uniquely designed to reflect what we wanted. Hers was a colourful, detailed protea with her dad's signature, a tribute to her late father. Mine was a black and grey protea covering my entire calf, symbolising resilience. It was significant, as I had just completed my first 100-miler.

These tattoos are more than ink on the skin; they are pieces of my life story—each representing a significant chapter, a reminder of who I am, what I've overcome, and the people and moments that matter most to me.

I love this saying:

**The Protea: It embodies the beauty of being resilient, courageous, strong, and full of hope.**

Saying farewell to friends, who are like family, takes work. I am incredibly blessed to have friendships that feel like lifelong connections, even if we've only known each other briefly. Rox, for instance, has become one of my closest friends and my best friend. We met just two years ago, in the middle of the second year of lockdown, but in that time, we've spent countless hours running side by side, sharing stories, and chasing dreams together. She has faced a tough year, and as we both sought a fresh start, I gently suggested we commemorate it with something permanent—a tattoo. She slowly warmed to the idea, and it soon became a reality.

Rox loves sunflowers. They're bright, vibrant, and full of life—just like her. As we brainstormed, we knew the sunflower would be at the centre of her tattoo. But the word that tied it all together for us was "journey." We had run the X-Berg adventure race together and needed a team name. Since we were in the Drakensberg, which translates to "Dragon Mountains," we settled on the name Ojekamanzi, meaning dragonfly. The dragonfly also became a symbol for us, representing transformation and adaptability.

Rox chose a small sunflower tattoo on her ankle, designed as a cross, with the word "journey" written along the stem. I went for a beautiful sunflower on my left forearm, with the same "journey" inscription, and a dragonfly on my ankle, symbolising the transformation we'd experienced together. Roxie's dragonfly might come later, but the sunflower was enough for now. I feel honoured to share this bond with her—her first tattoo marking a new chapter in our lives.

Some say tattoos are addictive. I don't believe I'm addicted. For me, it's about marking the moments that matter—wearing reminders of resilience, love, and the things that have shaped me. Life gives us scars without our choosing, reminders of the falls we've taken and the battles we've fought. Tattoos, however, are different. They are deliberate choices, symbols of what means the most to us. When I look down at my tattoos, I see the love of family, the strength of friendships, the goals I've chased, and the principles I strive to live by. And when life gets hard, those reminders anchor me—they tell me I have a purpose, that I am loved, and that better days are ahead.

### *I am resilient.*

*Writing these words has been challenging. In the process, I lost a dear friend, Grant Cummings, to tragedy. Grant was an integral part of my 100-mile journey. He meticulously worked out my race splits, cheered me on, and took much of the video footage that captured the highs and lows of the race. He was among the first to inspire me to dive deeper into trail running through the Trail Snakes community in the upper highway area. Losing him has been a profound shock, but in his memory, I find renewed strength. His legacy pushes me to keep going, share my story more boldly, and remind others that we become stronger through hard times. Grant, your presence is missed, but your impact remains. You've sparked a flame that will continue to burn brightly, encouraging others to be resilient, to chase their dreams, and to rise above.*

*I am resilient—and I will always carry that message forward.*

Not yet done…

### Thank you for being part of my journey.

I hope you've enjoyed reading about my adventures and that you've been re-ignited with a thirst for adventure and chasing your dreams. Each story, each chapter, was written to inspire you to dream big, embrace resilience, and pursue the extraordinary—because we all have a journey to share, and yours is just as important.

If this book has touched you in any way, I would appreciate a review on Amazon. I would love to hear your thoughts, reflections, and any feedback you have. Tag me on social media – @dawnnunesza on Instagram and Facebook – so I can hear from you directly! Your feedback means the world to me, and I am always open to questions and thoughts about the story.

You can reach me at:

- Instagram: dawnnunesza
- Facebook: dawnnunesza
- YouTube: DawnNunes

Thank you for taking the time to read my story. Your support and presence in this journey mean more than words can express.

For easy access to some of the fantastic groups and races mentioned in the book, scan the QR codes or check out the links below:

**Groups & Races**

**Fit4Rhino**                     Website: www.fit4rhinos.com

**UK WanderWomen**          Facebook: UK WanderWomen

Instagram: @ukwanderwomen

**WanderWomenKZN**    Instagram: @wanderwomenkzn

**13 Peaks Challenge**    Website: www.13peaks.co.za

13 PEAKS CHALLENGE

**Ultra-Trail Cape Town**    Website: www.ultratrailcapetown.com

UTCT

**Comrades Marathon**    www.comrades.com

COMRADES MARATHON

**Let's stay connected as we continue this incredible journey.**

**I would love to hear from you!**

# UTCT Kit and Nutrition Lists

## Kit for UTCT 100 Miler

Before diving into my gear, you must **check all mandatory items** for your specific race. These requirements are there for your safety, and you'll need to carry them throughout the race. Here's the kit I used for the Ultra-Trail Cape Town 100 miler:

- Waterproof Jacket with Taped Seams – First Ascent
- Buff
- Running Vest – RockRabbit
- Arm Sleeves
- Survival Blanket
- Whistle (attached to running vest)
- Charged Phone
- Headlamps – Ledlenser MH8 and Neo9R
- Adhesive Bandage
- Food Reserve
- Hydration (1.5-litre capacity)
- Personal Cup
- Race Number
- Peak Cap
- Cash
- Sunglasses
- Trail Shoes – Saucony Xodus
- Socks – Balega
- Powerbanks and Charging Cables
- Spare Hairband
- Watch – Garmin Fenix 6 with GPX map loaded
- Spare Batteries
- Poles – Aonijie
- Gloves
- GoPro
- Ziploc/Waterproof Bag for phone
- Strapping

# Nutrition for UTCT 100-Mile Race

Here's the fuel that kept me going through the highs and lows of the race:

- Pringles
- Hamburger (McDonald's, because why not?)
- Coffee (copious amounts)
- Speckled Eggs (jelly-centred chocolate confectionery)
- Watermelon
- Oranges
- Banana Bread
- Pancakes
- Noodles in Light Soup
- Millionaire Shortbread
- Mini Donuts
- Chicken Nuggets
- Meatballs
- Bar One (similar to a Mars bar)
- Custard and Jelly
- Baby Potatoes with Salt
- Bovril/Marmite Sandwiches
- Toffee
- Maurten Gels
- Tailwind
- Lekka (South African rehydrate)
- Coke and Water
- Salted Crackers
- Biltong (the best-dried meat in SA)
- Whey Protein Muscle Fuel
- Red Bull

This combination of gear and nutrition saw me through one of my life's most challenging and rewarding experiences. Stay prepared, stay fuelled, and you'll cross that finish line!

Front Cover

Sportograph UTCT

Back Cover

Peak Peeps Team 13 Peaks Challenge

Printed in Great Britain
by Amazon